CHRISTMAS IN FLORIDA

Santa takes a beach break.

CHRISTMAS IN FLORIDA

Kevin M. McCarthy

Pineapple Press, Inc.
Sarasota, Florida

Inquiries should be addressed to:

Pineapple Press, Inc.
P.O. Box 3899
Sarasota, Florida 34230

www.pineapplepress.com.

Library of Congress Cataloging-in-Publication Data

McCarthy, Kevin.
   Christmas in Florida / by Kevin M. McCarthy.—1st ed.
      p. cm.
   ISBN 1-56164-208-8 (pb : alk. paper)
      1. Christmas—Florida. 2. Florida—Social Life and customs. I. Title.
   GT4986.A2 F65 2000
   394.2663'09759—dc21

                                                                              00-034697

First Edition
10 9 8 7 6 5 4 3 2 1

Design by Shé Sicks
Printed and bound by Versa Press, Inc., in East Peoria, Illinois

CONTENTS

Introduction

Christmas and Florida—the two terms might not, at first glance, seem all that compatible. If one thinks only of snow and ice and the North Pole and sleighs, then the two do not go together. But if, when one conjures up images of Christmas, one thinks of families celebrating the birth of Christ in religious houses of worship, exchanging gifts with one another and the less fortunate, lighting Advent wreaths and Yule logs, caroling in the streets, and enjoying ethnic foods, then the two definitely can go together. If you add golf, tennis, fishing, swimming in outdoor pools and lakes, and shorts and sunglasses instead of ear muffs and several layers of clothing—then you have the best of two worlds: the warmth of both the holiday and the sun. What follows is the story of how Floridians have celebrated our most important holiday in the last four hundred years and how countless residents and visitors from near and abroad have adapted the holiday celebrations to the waterways of south Florida, the citrus groves of central Florida, the pine trees of north Florida, and the beaches of the Panhandle.

My first Christmas in Florida was one of my all-time best. I had spent twenty-three years in the cold of New Jersey and New York, two years in the very un-Christian-like atmosphere of Moslem Turkey in the Middle East, and four years in the North Carolina cities of Chapel Hill and Raleigh. In 1969, I turned down a position at a university in upstate Minnesota and moved down to Gainesville to begin teaching at the University of Florida. There, on that first Christmas Eve, my wife gave birth to our first son, Brendan. As I listened to the late-late television news in the hospital, I heard the announcer end his broadcast by telling all of us Floridians that the coldest place in the country that night was in upstate Minnesota. "I could have been up there, shivering the night away. Instead, here I am in warm, sunny Florida," I thought gleefully. It was a contrast I have felt keenly in the years since that wonderful night.

What follows are stories of what Christmas has been like in the Sunshine State over the past four centuries, based on reports of missionaries, explorers, historians, and reporters. Also included are Christmas recipes native to a state better known for its alligators than its pheasants and for its citrus than its eggnog. The book begins by describing Christmas in the South: how Southerners celebrate the season differently than Northerners do and how the observance of Christmas this century has changed over the decades. The final section includes eight Christmas stories set in Florida.

Although visitors and new residents to Florida may pine for the snow and mistletoe of a Northern Christmas (perhaps forgetting about the miseries of suffering from colds, driving on icy roads, shoveling driveways over and over again, bundling up children for outside play, and then soon unbundling them), a Florida Christmas is probably closer to the original one in Bethlehem in terms of weather and topography. In the twentieth century, as Florida came to resemble the rest of the nation in many ways, the state still retained its idiosyncratic ways of celebrating the season — for example, by having Santa arrive by boat and even seaplane instead of by sleigh. As we enter the twenty-first century, Floridians have definitely entered the mainstream of America, especially as second- and third-generation children of immigrants choose New World customs over those of the Old World.

As you read the following chapters, perhaps in the warmth of a sunny day on a boat in the Gulf or on a beach in the Keys, keep a warm feeling for those less fortunate, i.e., non-Floridians up north.

Acknowledgments

I wish to thank the following individuals for their help in this project: Alyson Alpert, Sandra Bogan, Elizabeth Briggs, Liisa Collins, Robena Cornwell, Jim Crane, Jim Cusick, Jack Ewing, Franz Futterknecht, Jean Holzapfel, Margaret Hostetler, Bart Hudson, Nicholas Kontaridis, Harold Nugent, Laurent Pellerin, Rosa Piedra, Vickie Prewett, C. L. Rose, Ulla Saari, Sharon Smith, John Van Hook, Christine Vargas, and Jerry Wilkinson.

Delivering presents in the heat of the South can tire out Santa.

EARLY CHRISTMAS CELEBRATIONS IN THE SOUTH

In the United States, Christmas has not always been the happy holiday that we now usually associate the day with. For example, the early Protestants of New England generally discouraged the celebration of the birth of Christ, associating it with the Catholic church. But Southerners disagreed with their Northern cousins and made the day into a family-centered, joyous occasion. True, the farming families of the South did not look on the day so much as a religious holiday as a social time, but they did continue such European customs as decorating their houses with flowers and shrubs, burning the Yule log, and singing carols.

Floridians can decorate their trees with shells at Christmastime.
Florida State Archives

Southerners have always managed to adapt to local conditions. For example, they substituted seafood and turkey for the more traditional European dishes of goose and beef; Southern pine trees for European cedars and firs; and Spanish moss, seashells, and sand dollars for tinsel and other decorations. The wealthier Southerners even went fox hunting on Christmas morning.

While New England Protestants, especially the Puritans, had Christmas banned in the Massachusetts Bay Colony in 1659, Southern states such as Alabama, Arkansas, and Louisiana became the first in the nation to declare Christmas a legal holiday, although it did not become a federal holiday until 1870,

13

seven years after Thanksgiving had earned that honor. The most southern state of all, at least in terms of geography, was Florida, a land settled by Spanish Catholics and therefore even more willing to celebrate the nativity of Christ than New England states. Florida established Christmas as a legal holiday in 1881.

Because many in the South were farmers, the Christmas season came at a good time of the year, after the busy fall harvest was in and before the colder, quieter days of January and February arrived. In fact, Southerners sometimes extended the festivities over the whole week from Christmas to New Year's, sometimes even as far as the Epiphany (January 6). Indeed, parts of North Carolina actually celebrated Christmas on January 5, following a tradition practiced before the switch from the Gregorian to the Julian calendar in 1752.

The tradition of celebrating Christmas on antebellum Southern plantations extended back to the early 1800s. Many in the South followed English customs, especially those of the Episcopalian religion. Plantation owners often staged elaborate Christmas parties, and although slaves did not take part in those parties, they were able to have an extended holiday from work.

The South added its own touch to these celebrations in terms of food, the Christmas tree, and the Yule log. Southerners preferred dishes such as turkey, ham, goose, and mincemeat pies. A particular favorite, pecans, which are grown in commercial Southern groves and in private yards, have been an important part of the South's culinary fare, whether in pralines or fruit cakes or pecan pies. Even alcoholic drinks such as brandy, rum punch, and wine were in great supply at that time of the year and became associated with Christmas.

The Southern tradition of setting off firecrackers on Christmas began with the French in Louisiana. The tradition of shooting off firearms and firecrackers, something that Floridians also enjoyed (see next chapter), may have originated from the practice of neighbors sending Christmas greetings to those on nearby farms or from the superstition of warding off evil spirits. Doing so was a relatively inexpensive way to greet the holidays, and one that always garnered attention.

The Christmas tree, one of the most popular symbols of the Christmas season, has strong ties to the South. North Carolina has produced more Christmas trees for the White House than any other state and continues to lead the nation in the production of Christmas trees for sale in many parts of the country. The South may have been the first place in the United States that used such a tree as part of the Yuletide celebration. Historians trace the custom back to the 1752 migration of Moravians from Pennsylvania to Old Salem (later Winston-Salem), North Carolina. In 1801, some Moravian missionaries who had gone to Georgia invited local Cherokee Indians to join them in celebrating Christmas. The "Christmas tree" that the missionaries cut down may have been one of the earliest uses of a tree in such a celebration.

In 1842, a German immigrant named Charles Minnegerode decorated a fir tree in Williamsburg, Virginia, using popcorn strands, nuts, and pieces of colored paper. It would take another thirty years before Christmas trees became prevalent in the South. In the decades after the Civil War, Southerners used such trees on a regular basis, often decorating them with local materials such as seashells, or magnolia leaves, dried hydrangeas, holly berries, and Spanish moss. In the 1870s, they also used toy-shaped ornaments imported from Germany and later mass-produced decorations from mail-order houses. They also decorated their houses using berries, mistletoe, and pinecones.

Today, for many in the South and elsewhere, the Christmas tree is the center of secular celebrations as family members put their presents under it and their decorations on it. Children especially equate the tree with the Yuletide season since the tree is often in the most important part of the house, is more meaningful than carols or food, and grows in importance as the number of presents under it grows.

Floridians have been known to put their Christmas trees in unusual places.
Florida State Archives

The Yule log, thought by some to force the Devil out of the house with its fumes, was one of the customs the English brought to the New World. On Southern plantations, the slaves would keep the log, cut from a sturdy tree, burning for over a week, since the master often promised the slaves that they did not have to work in the fields for as long as the log burned. Some of the early settlers kept part of the log for the following Christmas as a sign of good luck.

Southern communities, like those elsewhere, have struggled with the commercialization of the holiday. While editorialists continue to urge a return to old-fashioned values ("Put Christ back in Christmas" and "Share your Christmas dinner with those less fortunate"), our market economies will probably prevail. The Christmas shopping season begins the day after Thanksgiving, and shoppers receive constant reminders of how many shopping days until Christmas. Stores can make as much as twenty-five percent of their annual income in that month.

The season can bring out the best in people. Many newspapers feature a "hard-luck case of the day" in order to raise funds for that family. Such newspapers as Jacksonville's *Times-Union* and Gainesville's *Sun* describe the plight of the less fortunate, followed by a predicted outpouring of generous donations. Many towns go back in time to recreate old-time Christmases. For example, Amelia Island has a Victorian Seaside Christmas, and Lightner Museum in St. Augustine has exhibits about Christmases long past.

And, of course, Florida newspapers delight in reminding readers just how cold it is in Minnesota or upstate New York, wherever visitors are liable to be from. Somehow the mention of blizzards and ice storms and impassable roads makes the hearts of Floridians that much warmer.

CHRISTMAS CELEBRATIONS IN FLORIDA OVER THE YEARS

Although the Florida Legislature didn't establish Christmas as a legal holiday until 1881, Floridians celebrated the holiday in different ways up until the twentieth century, when better transportation and communication decreased the isolation of the peninsula and saw the state enter the mainstream of American life. This trend has continued to the present, as transplants from elsewhere continue to move here, averaging an amazing eight hundred to nine hundred people a day.

What follows are selections from early Florida newspapers, diaries, and other accounts of how Floridians have celebrated what is clearly the most important public holiday of the year. The cross-sampling is probably typical of how many towns and cities in the Spanish and British colonies and American territory spent the day.

TALLAHASSEE (1539)
FIRST CHRISTMAS MASS IN AMERICA

When Hernando de Soto arrived in Tampa Bay in 1539, he could not have imagined what sights he would see and what difficulties he would encounter over the next year. He and his troops came ashore someplace in the Tampa Bay area, probably near the mouth of the Little Manatee River, and began marching north through present-day Dade City, Ocala, Gainesville, Lake City, and Live Oak. When they arrived in the vicinity of Tallahassee in the fall of 1539, they came upon an Apalachee village, quickly drove out the Indians, stole their supply of food, and set up defenses against the natives, who continued to harass and kill them. Winter had overtaken the party, and de Soto decided to spend the time in the Indian village of Anhayea in the center of Apalachee territory. De Soto's group remained in the area until March 1540, when they resumed their ill-fated search for gold and other precious metals.

In late December 1539, the soldiers and their leader wanted to take time out from their trek to celebrate the birth of Christ the way they had back in Catholic Spain. That first Christmas Day in Florida was cold and miserable, conditions that matched the mood of the Europeans. The Spanish soldiers were far from home and their loved ones. They had been searching for silver and gold for months but had little or nothing to show for their efforts. The Native Americans continued to be hostile, attacking them and killing the less careful soldiers.

In what is today called the Governor Martin Site, about one half mile from the Capitol building, the Spanish gathered around the twelve Roman Catholic priests who had accompanied the expedition and participated in the first Christmas celebration in the New World. After celebrating the Latin Mass and singing some favorite hymns, they would all no doubt have had a small feast, although they probably would not have exchanged gifts under those harsh circumstances. The expedition still had a long way to go before their exploration was finished, and many would die on the way, including de Soto.

Today, visitors can see the site of that first Christmas at the Governor Martin Site, which is located at 1022 Desoto Park Drive, east of the Capitol and off Lafayette Street, which is parallel to Apalachee Parkway.

Modern Floridians re-enact the first Christmas celebration in the New World.
Florida State Archives

ST. AUGUSTINE (1565)
EARLY CELEBRATIONS OF THE HOLIDAY

Twenty-six years after de Soto's expedition, Pedro Menéndez de Avilés established Spain's permanent foothold in the New World when he founded the settlement of St. Augustine. While no records seem to exist that describe the first Christmas in St. Augustine (or St. Augustin, as it was then called) after the Spanish arrived in 1565, historians speculate that they would have celebrated the Nativity of Christ, *Fiesta de Natividad*, there as they had in Spain, namely as a religious holiday. That would have meant that all those who could would have attended Mass that day. Because the Spanish arrived in Florida in the fall of that year, they might not have had time to make the usual preparations, but they surely would have emphasized the religious aspects of the holiday.

FLORIDA'S EAST COAST (1696)
SHIPWRECKED QUAKERS

A young merchant, Jonathan Dickinson, and his party of Quakers were shipwrecked near present-day Jupiter Inlet in September 1696 while they were sailing from Port Royal, Jamaica, to Philadelphia, Pennsylvania. As they made their way north along the east coast of Florida, they came upon many different bands of Native Americans, some friendly and some hostile. Dickinson described the long walk back to South Carolina, including a particularly hard 230 miles from Jupiter Island to St. Augustine, in his remarkable book entitled *God's Protecting Providence. Being the Narrative of a Journey from Port Royal in Jamaica to Philadelphia between August 23, 1696 and April 1, 1697.*

On Christmas Day, he noted that Spanish soldiers were "tinkling on a piece of iron and singing," making do with the sparse materials available on the Spanish frontier. Dickinson also mentioned that the Spanish soldiers and Native Americans were begging from one, which was reminiscent of the old Spanish custom of *pidiendo aguinaldo,* or asking for small gifts from others. The soldiers probably also engaged in some kind of gambling, probably with cards. Its popular counterpart today is playing the Christmas lottery in Spain and Spanish-American countries. One can only imagine how happy the shipwrecked survivors were that Christmastime when they finally reached the safety of north Florida, Georgia, and South Carolina before returning to Philadelphia.

ST. AUGUSTINE (1700s)
SPANISH CELEBRATIONS OF CHRISTMAS

Because the Spanish explorers were Catholic, their celebrations of Christmas were quite different from the Protestant celebrations further to the north in the thirteen colonies founded by the English. The Spanish Catholics, especially the devout ones, would have made the Mass the central part of their festivities. As in places such as Texas, also settled by the Spanish, the white settlers in St. Augustine might have reenacted the journey of the wise men to Bethlehem, perhaps enlisting some local Native Americans to fill out the numbers.

As time went on and the Spanish settled into the town, they probably would have gone down to the local marketplace around Christmastime and bought a *nacimiento,* or nativity, to display in their homes. The set would have consisted of a group of figures, often made of clay, representing the baby Jesus, Mary, Joseph, maybe even the ox and mule in a manger, although the manger became more popular in later centuries.

The better-off families among the Spanish would have set aside a whole room in their home to display the manger, along with imitation sheep, shepherds, rocks, and mountains and many candles. As described in Charles Kany's *Life and Manners in Madrid, 1750–1800* (1932), most of the Spanish in St. Augustine would go out in search of the usual *aguinaldo,* or Christmas present, which might be candles, chocolate, or silver coins.

Christmas Eve would have been the time to entertain one's friends. The wealthier would be expected to repeat their sumptuous dinners the next day too. Among the guests would be those who had attended the ladies' *tertulias,* evening gatherings, during the previous year. According to church custom, the faithful were not supposed to eat meat on Christmas Eve, since it was considered a day of abstinence, but many, if not most, Spanish tended to ignore such admonitions and to eat what they wanted.

Those who followed Spanish customs of the time were sure to pay many visits to friends and acquaintances on Christmas Day itself, or at least to send notes or cards to wish the recipients a Merry Christmas. The real gift giving would be done on January 6, the Day of the Three Kings. As that day approached, the children would take pleasure in moving the three wise men and their camels closer to the nativity scene. On the eve of that holiday, the children would place shiny shoes filled with hay near the manger where the three kings would be sure to see them. If the children had been good the previous year, the camels would somehow eat the hay in the shoes and the three kings would leave behind some gifts.

ST. AUGUSTINE (1702)
THE BRITISH LAY SIEGE TO THE TOWN

When the British in the original thirteen colonies attempted to end the Spanish foothold south of them, Governor James Moore led a force of five hundred to six hundred Carolina militia and three hundred to six hundred Native Americans south to the capital of the Spanish colony: St. Augustine. At that time, the little settlement had about nine hundred residents and only about three hundred soldiers able to defend the outpost. When the British forces arrived in the town in early November 1702, they found that the inhabitants had taken shelter inside the Castillo de San Marcos, the large stone fort near the water. The British guns were not heavy enough to destroy the fort, and the Spanish did not have enough troops to drive off the invaders, so both sides settled down for what might be a long siege.

Charles Arnade, in *The Siege of St. Augustine in 1702* (1959), described Christmas Eve as a night when the Spanish huddled within the safety of the Castillo while British soldiers hunkered down outside its walls. Inside, Governor Zúñiga, in trying to keep some semblance of normality, had the soldiers and townspeople play their *vihuelas* (guitars) and mouth harps in a Christmas Eve party. He wanted to boost the morale of the people at a time normally set aside for holiday celebrations but one that then seemed very threatening to the Spanish in the fort. Zúñiga also ordered the treasurer and the accountant to distribute a Christmas bonus to the soldiers. When the two officials protested that the fort could not afford such generosity, the governor told them to charge the amount to the following year's account because the soldiers needed to be cheered up at that critical time.

On Christmas Day, two British ships arrived off the harbor with reinforcements and more ammunition. With the increased ability of the British to bombard the Castillo, the Spanish who huddled inside the fort were terrified of what lay ahead. The Spanish governor, fearing that panic was about to break out among his people, forbade any discussion of the military predicament. For some reason, the British postponed their attack, perhaps hoping for more ships to join them.

On the day after Christmas, the Spanish were ecstatic when lookouts spotted four Spanish ships approaching from Cuba. In the next week, when the British realized that their vessels were trapped in the harbor, they burned four of their ships to keep them out of the hands of the Spanish, abandoned four others, set fire to the town of St. Augustine, and marched north to safety. The little Spanish town was in ashes, but at least it had been saved from the British and could be rebuilt. It had been a Christmas season that the besieged Spanish would not soon forget.

ST. AUGUSTINE (1763–1783)
THE BRITISH CONTROL FLORIDA

When the British gained control of Florida and forced the Spanish to leave for Cuba in 1763, the new rulers no doubt would have followed as closely as possible those customs they remembered from England. Some of the wealthier British settlers would have decorated their houses with fruit, holly, laurel, and mistletoe. Those who wanted to decorate a tree would have most likely brought it inside on Christmas Eve and kept it there until January 6, the Feast of the Epiphany or Twelfth Night. Setting it up earlier than Christmas Eve or taking it down before Twelfth Night might, according to the more superstitious, bring on bad luck.

According to W. Carew Hazlitt's *Faiths and Folklore* (1905) and R. Chambers' *Book of Days* (1878), both about eighteenth-century England, the British living in St. Augustine might have observed some customs from home. For example, those from the north of England would try to grab an extended apple with only their mouths after tying their hands behind their backs. A superstition in some parts of the country was that the first person who entered a house on Christmas and New Year's mornings should have dark hair. This was based on the belief that Judas had red hair and therefore red-haired people were to be avoided. The soldiers probably engaged in some kind of sports during the holidays. Also, it was customary for British officers to give gifts to those lower in rank. If possible, the British would have had roast beef and plum pudding for their main meal, as well as a special Christmas pie made with chicken, eggs, sugar, currants, citron, orange peel, and various spices.

The British would have also gone caroling from house to house, especially on Christmas Eve, as they went through the streets guided only by a few lanterns. The season was supposed to be a time when people forgot their quarrels, renewed old friendships, and generally behaved well toward one another. They would have paid special care to the needs of the poor, particularly with regard to food and clothes.

To this day, the people of St. Augustine often reenact in the early part of December a British Night Watch Ceremony, a secular custom that bridges the gap between Thanksgiving and Christmas. In that living-history demonstration, which involves townspeople and the military, officials close the city gates and participants carry torches, as the British did in the eighteenth century on their nightly rounds to secure St. Augustine's walls. Today, the singing of Christmas carols winds up the ceremony and adds a religious touch.

ST. AUGUSTINE (1790)
REBEL PRISONER

Josiah Smith, a South Carolina prisoner in St. Augustine in 1790, wrote a diary about his imprisonment and described a Christmas celebration that December: "Being Christmas Day, a very good dinner of roasted turkeys and pig, corn'd beef, ham, plumb pudding and pumpkin tarts, etc. was provided by our Mess [people who regularly ate together] and having invited the Mess at Parole Corner to partake thereof, we dined together, thirty in number, very heartily, and many of the Company as merrily spent the evening by a variety of songs, etc."

As more and more Americans moved into north Florida and as the Spanish hold on the territory weakened, the settlers slowly began to Americanize the towns and even holidays such as Christmas. However, the legacy of Spanish missions and the strong Catholic presence in north Florida have made religious customs a strong part of local festivities to this day.

PENSACOLA (1822)
MARDI GRAS AND THE FEAST OF ST. STEPHEN

Early Pensacola during the territorial days (from 1821, when the United States purchased Florida from Spain, until 1845, when Florida became a state) was greatly influenced by the Spanish, who had controlled the peninsula for most of the previous two centuries. Local revelers in Pensacola, perhaps influenced by the French presence to the west, managed to combine Christmas celebrations with those of Mardi Gras, the prelude to Lent, which meant that the city had a festive mood from early December until the beginning of Lent in the spring.

One American Army officer stationed in Pensacola, Lt. George McCall, wrote letters home in 1822 that described how the local Creoles combined Christmas celebrations with those of the Feast of St. Stephen (December 26). The season was opened with a masked ball and continued with many parties in an effort to have "a season from which care should be banished, and over which pleasure should preside." The increasing number of Americans were only too willing to take part in Carnival, thus combining the best of several cultures.

Christmas dinner for the officers in Pensacola often consisted of roast turkey, plum pudding, and gumbo soup, a combination of dried and powdered sassafras leaves and chicken or oyster soup. Because Pensacola was a thriving port, its residents had many imports to choose from, including a wide variety of alcoholic beverages ranging from absinthe to gin to whiskey. The men could also smoke genuine "Havana segars" after the meal. Those who ate or drank too much over the holidays could try a quick cure from the fluid extract of sarsaparilla, which was supposed to cure any and all illnesses known to mankind. Some of the young belles who spent almost every night of the long season dancing and partying later became much more religious, centering their Christmas celebrations around the church and family.

NEAR BUSHNELL (1835)
THE DADE MASSACRE

Christmas Day 1835 turned out to be a particularly bad time for many of the white settlers and soldiers in Florida. As tensions rose between the whites and the Native Americans, conflict seemed inevitable. On December 25, 1835, the Seminoles raided sugar plantations along the east coast of Florida around Daytona and further south. The Native Americans burned all the buildings in New Smyrna and did so much damage to the nearby plantations that some of them were never cultivated again.

A St. Augustine monument to the soldiers in Major Dade's troop that were killed.
Florida State Archives

When Maj. Francis Dade and his two companies of soldiers headed off from Fort Brooke in Tampa in late December for the long, overland trek to Fort King in Ocala, they had mixed feelings. Even though it was the Christmas season, they had a difficult journey to make. And, in fact, they never made it to Fort King. Near present-day Bushnell, three days after Christmas, a band of Seminoles ambushed them and killed all but three of the 111 soldiers, including Major Dade. This precipitated the Second Seminole War and the slaughter or deportation of hundreds of Seminoles.

LAKE OKEECHOBEE (1837)
FEDERAL TROOPS ROUT THE SEMINOLES

For two years after the Dade Massacre, federal troops chased the elusive Seminoles throughout Florida, seldom encountering them in fixed battles but instead fighting a guerilla war with Native Americans who knew the land well and were defending their homeland.

Finally, on Christmas Day 1837, federal troops under Col. (later President) Zachary Taylor defeated four hundred Seminoles in the largest and one of the most important battles of the Second Seminole War. At a site near Lake Okeechobee, marked today by a plaque indicating National Register status, both sides fought the only pitched battle of that war on, of all ironies, a day known to many peoples as one of "peace on earth, good will toward men." Although the war would drag on for another four years, those federal troops effectively ended large-scale resistance by the Seminoles, who were reluctant to stand and fight, knowing that they could ill afford to lose many Indians to the seemingly endless supply of white soldiers.

AROUND ST. AUGUSTINE (1838)
SEMINOLE THREATS

Christmas in North Florida in the 1830s was a difficult time for the white settlers, who often felt threatened by the Native Americans who controlled much of the countryside. Just three years after the Dade Massacre, *The News* of St. Augustine had dire warnings of impending doom in its Christmas edition of 1838:

> This is the third [Christmas] which has come round since Florida has been the theatre of war. Time has here gathered many familiar faces to their final account, whilst our red neighbors have sent prematurely numerous victims to the tomb. Our last "merry making" was on the banks of

> Lake Harney, and with our usual sanguineness, we then
> looked to a comfortable dinner, in the quietude of peace,
> in 1838. Vain and presumptuous longing—the dinner
> was most excellent, but the Indian is still unchecked—and
> we will wager an old coat that things will be even worse
> December 25, 1839.

The writer was partly right. The Second Seminole War, which dragged on until 1842, was the longest, bloodiest, and most expensive Indian war in the history of our nation. The Third Seminole War broke out in 1855 and lasted for three years.

KEYS (1830s)
CHRISTMAS ON INDIAN KEY

Although the Florida Keys were sparsely settled by non-Indians in the first half of the nineteenth century, those who did live there tried to maintain the trappings of civilization as best they could. According to historian Jerry Wilkinson of the Historical Preservation Society of the Upper Keys, the first mention of Christmas there was in a diary entry by Key West attorney William Hackley for December 25, 1830:

> About 20 persons sat down to dinner at Mr. Pinkhams.
> The two Mrs. Wescotts and Mrs. Pinkham and Miss
> Foote sat down to the table. It is the first time I have eaten
> dinner in the company of ladies on this key. Several of the
> party got a little merry, but not much so. There were per-
> sons parading the streets till a late hour firing guns and
> whooping and hollering in honor of the day.

When famed botanist Dr. Henry Perrine and his family arrived at Indian Key on Christmas Day eight years later, Perrine's daughter described Jacob Housman, a wrecker and entrepreneur who was influential enough to have Dade County established in 1836 and Indian Key named as its county seat:

> As soon as our vessel came to anchor, Mr. [Charles] Howe
> came on board, and in his boat we landed. Our first
> Christmas dinner was eaten at his hospitable table. How
> well I remember the curious Conch soup, and that roast
> beef!!
>
> Some years before Captain Houseman [sic], the owner
> of the Island, had imported a cow and bull, hoping to

raise stock. For some reason the cow died, and he had determined to kill the bull, but hearing that father was coming, determined to await his arrival so that we should enjoy what was to be to them, such a great luxury! forgetting that we were from the land of beef.

The task Mr. Howe had in cutting that roast, and our teeth had in masticating it, can better be imagined than told!! (If it was not one of the creatures turned out of the Ark, it must have been a near descendant!!) But the fresh vegetables & delicious fruits made amends. I cannot forget our delight on first seeing this beautiful little island of only 12 acres.

The Native Americans, angered at outrages committed against them by Jacob Housman, attacked the white residents of Indian Key in 1840. They killed Dr. Perrine, but Housman managed to escape.

PENSACOLA (1841)
DON'T FORGET THE POOR

The *Pensacola Gazette*'s issue on December 26, 1841, reminded readers not to forget their less-fortunate neighbors:

A merry Christmas to our readers, and to all, the summer is past, the autumn has come and gone, and we are again at that peculiarly festive season of the year whose annual return should open the hand of bounty to the poor, and in this land of the peace and plenty at least, fill the heart of gratitude to God. Even here, however, we are not without suffering; sometimes the offspring of misfortune, but almost always the consequences of vice or crime. In other countries, whole classes of people are born to suffering, are the heirs of privation, and have nothing but this to transmit to their offspring. Here as a general rule, none are very poor but by their own fault; yet even to them, let the hand of bounty be opened for they are our brothers and we are but stewards, owning nothing of ourselves but enjoying everything that we have, at the will of the eternal source of all benevolence. Let those who have abundance then, give something to gladden the hearts of poor neighbors and let the master extend his bounty to the slave . . . so shall we indeed have a merry Christmas.

ST. AUGUSTINE (1842)
A RESPITE FROM THE INDIAN WAR

The 1842 holiday season, while still full of attacks in the Second Seminole War, would see the end of that conflict. Although war would flare up again in the following decade, all had hopes in 1842 that this peace would bring an everlasting end to the hostilities. As happened elsewhere in frontier territories, Floridians somehow united over their celebration of Christmas and even used the occasion to lay down the plow and thoroughly enjoy themselves, at least for a day or that week before New Year's Day. The editor and publisher of the *St. Augustin News*, Thomas Russell, wrote the following about the season in 1842:

> Eyes beam more brightly and look more kindly...even the household dog wags his tail with additional pleasure. Then too, the preparation of turkey and minced pies, and that nectar and delight—eggnog—a drink that seems only allowable at Christmas . . . then there is the interchange of visits . . . telling choice legends around the fire.
>
> Christmas! How our memories travel back to this delightful season when our only ambition was to make a noise by firing a pop gun, stay our ravenous appetites with mince pies, and answer, like good Christians, all the questions of the Catechism . . . these were the aspirations of childhood.

ST. AUGUSTINE (1844)
MASQUERADING

A young man who would later become a Presbyterian bishop in Minnesota, Henry Benjamin Whipple traveled through the South, including Florida, in 1843 and 1844. While in north Florida in December 1843 and January 1844, he witnessed in St. Augustine what he called "masquerading," an event that began at Christmastime and continued until Lent. Based on the old Spanish custom of Carnival, the so-called masquers in their disguises—which might be of older people, both hideous and fashionable, Native American and European—went from house to house to act out various parts, sometimes accompanied by musical instruments such as a tambourine or violin. They sometimes sent word ahead that they would dance at a certain house in the evening. The owner of the house then provided some refreshments. The residents in St. Augustine slowly substituted new American customs and amusements for the older, Spanish ones.

PENSACOLA (1845)
CHRISTMAS AFTER FLORIDA BECAME A STATE

In the year that Florida entered the Union as the twenty-seventh state, the editor of the *Pensacola Gazette* (December 27, 1845) referred to the good times people usually experienced at that time of the year, but he also showed a weariness. He wrote the following:

> As Christmas comes but once a year, our readers must excuse the absence of editorial matter this week. We are not in the vein to write about any thing, and least of all about the holy-day feeling of festivity manifested all around us. Not to sympathize with the joys of others is selfish and unsocial, it is true, and yet, as we go along through life, and the novelty and romance of this anniversary of fun and frolic and good dinners wears away, it really comes to be matter of doubt whether its annoyances are not about equivalent to its enjoyments; so that there is, perhaps, the greater necessity for wishing to every body—a merry christmas and a happy new year.

ORLANDO (1850s)
CELEBRATIONS

E. H. Grove described in *From Florida Sand to "the City Beautiful"* (1949) the celebrations held in Orlando in the 1850s. Early settlers spent the day feasting, dancing, and, once the churches were organized, attending religious services. Because most people did not have much money, gifts were modest: red hair ribbons for the girls and white, sticky candy for all the children. The women enjoyed their snuff, the men their tobacco.

Some of the residents would have the local "Crackers" over for dinner on Christmas Day. So many wild turkeys were available in the woods that people would kill more birds than they could use right away. At a time when no ice or cold storage was available, they would dry the turkey breasts for future use. The main Christmas meal would consist of bear and deer meat, sweet potatoes, homemade cheese, corn bread, and lots of syrup made from sugar cane. Or they might barbecue a hog or steer or cook fish.

The more mischievous boys would build a fort out of boxes and place it across South Orange Avenue, forcing pedestrians to detour around the block near Court Street. One time the boys let a young calf loose on the second floor of the Lucky Hotel. Another time they built a fire around a sleeping drunken man; when his coat caught on fire, they had to douse the flames and treat his burns.

When Billy Bowlegs and some of his Seminoles showed up, intent on seeking what Grove called "fire water," they were sent to the old courthouse, where some Presbyterian ladies, who were holding a bazaar, gave them a good dinner, though they were somewhat afraid of the Indians. The next day the Indians disappeared into the forest.

When some cowboys showed up late at night, the marshall let them have their fun, mostly because they greatly outnumbered him. The cowboys rode up and down the street, firing their pistols into the air; they even rode their horses into both bars in town and drank their liquor without dismounting. One of the men, spying something "fancy" on the wall, shot three bullets into the object. Others lassoed a cow and dragged it through town, then tried lassoing each other or any pedestrian they came upon. The more sedate citizens of the young town were no doubt glad when the Christmas holidays ended and people could get back to the ordinary.

TAMPA (1855)
TENSE TIMES

Christmas Day in 1855 in the area around Tampa was a tense time. The Seminoles had attacked settlements in the previous weeks and seemed intent on reigniting the war with federal troops. Two Seminole Indian wars had already been fought and a third one seemed imminent, especially after the settlers heard about an Indian slaughter of soldiers near Ft. Myers. Young men waged mock battles with the Native Americans, firing many rounds at the imaginary foe. Meanwhile, residents were out signing up volunteers for the expected battle with the Seminoles. At a church service in Tampa on Christmas Eve 1855, the minister prayed "to God to stop the war and bloodshed almost at the hearthstones and to cause the troubled elements, now afar in the land, to be calm." That afternoon, Tampa residents had held a mass meeting at the county courthouse. A lawyer of the town, Colonel Magbee, had railed against the Native Americans and urged all his listeners to fight against them, driving them out of Florida and to the West.

The Third Seminole War would begin that year and drag on for three years, after which most of the remaining Indians would be shipped to Indian Territory in what is today Oklahoma. About three hundred

Seminoles fled into the Florida Everglades in south Florida, where federal troops were reluctant to go. Today, the three thousand descendants of those Seminoles are prospering in Florida.

PENSACOLA (1857)
CHRISTMAS GOODS FOR SALE

The *Pensacola Gazette* on December 12, 1857, had the following items listed for sale at Alex Bright's store on Palafox Street:

Ladies Chenille Scarfs	80 cents
Ladies Plush Scarfs	50 cents
Petersham capes and collars	$2.00
Jaconet collars	6 to 20 cents
Silver plated napkin rings	30 cents
Ivory nut toys, all kinds	10 cents
Elegant cameo setts [sic]	$10.00
Gold Stone setts [sic]	5,6 and 7 dollars
Variety of Ladies breast pins	$2.00 to $5.00

The ad also noted "Bracelets, signet rings, scarf pins—all at lowest rates. ALSO—Lot elegant CREVATS for gentlemen. Call soon and secure a BARGAIN."

NORTH FLORIDA (1860s)
SLAVE PLANTATIONS

Julia Floyd Smith wrote in her *Slavery and Plantation Growth in Antebellum Florida, 1821-1860* (1973) how the slaves often celebrated Christmas. As was true in other Southern states, plantation owners in Florida usually allowed slaves free days on and after Christmas, sometimes extending the holidays to New Year's Day. One plantation overseer gave each of his slaves a pound of pork on Christmas Day, while other slave owners spread out a large dinner on tables under the trees near the slave quarters and gave the men liquor and the women clothes and shoes.

At one plantation in north Florida, the wife of the slave owner began in the fall making a Christmas list for slaves. After the cotton crop had been harvested, the owner sent the list to stores in New York. In due time, the presents—dresses, shawls, hats, and shoes for the women, overcoats and boots for the men—arrived at the plantation, to be distributed to the slaves on Christmas Day, a respite from the long days they worked in the fields the rest of the year. The threat to withhold presents from the more recalcitrant slaves was probably a strong motivation for all to behave themselves in the month or two leading up to Christmas.

ST. AUGUSTINE (1863)
THE CIVIL WAR

Although the Civil War did not affect Florida as severely as it did other Southern states, the effective Union blockade caused hardships and constraints. Many items were in short supply, and Christmas had to be celebrated in a more subdued way than in antebellum days. Gifts were usually homemade, and all food was grown in local gardens. Even so, a St. Augustine resident wrote the following in 1863:

> We attended a party last evening at Miss Mathers. We had
> a nice Christian dinner. A nice roast duck, the last of the
> flock, some chicken salad and a pie for dessert, fruit, but
> it remained untouched. Our dinner was not elaborate but
> good. . . .

Lt. J. H. Linsley, who was stationed in St. Augustine that December, mentioned that a week after Christmas the locals celebrated the emancipation of the slaves:

> Anniversary of President's proclamation of Freedom cele-
> brated by Freedmen of Florida. Addresses on the Plaza by
> Anti Slavery men of New England to the negroes of this
> slave ridden state of Florida. Music by the colored schools
> who came out in procession in gala dress. Winding up
> with fine collation provided by the colored people, to
> which the army officers of both regiments and the hospi-
> tal and others were invited.

ST. AUGUSTINE (1866)
AFTER THE CIVIL WAR

The sense of relief people felt after the Civil War was apparent in news accounts of the 1866 Christmas celebration, as in this excerpt from the *St. Augustine Examiner* (December 29, 1866):

> For many years the coming of grey bearded Santa Claus
> has not been celebrated with so much joy and relish by all
> sexes and ages of our citizens as it was on Monday Eve and

Tuesday [December 24 and 25]. If we may employ a slight exaggeration of terms, we should say that the dwellings in every street opened their wide doors to the hospitalities of the season, and where clouds of gloom had long overhung the domestic hearth, they were on this day and Eve dispelled in the universal mirth and happiness.

The midnight mass at the Catholic Church was unusually grand and impressive. Hardly had the ancient bells pealed out the midnight hour, when the church presented a most glorious picture. The holy strains of song and chant, the high altar with its brilliant illuminations and tasteful decoration, the crowded interior, and the solemnity of the hour and the event lent a holy glory to the scene.

The Festival at the Court House on Monday Eve was a fine success. The delicacy of female taste gave a charm to all arrangements, and the children especially were delighted and made happy.

The Freedmen's Fair at St. Mary's Convent on Wednesday evening was just as successful and enjoyable. It received the support which it merited.

The masquerade on Wednesday afternoon was a jolly feature of the day and afforded much innocent diversion.

In proportion to the quantity of amusement, we believe that very little disorder occurred. May the new year be as full of joy and prosperity to all of us, as our Christmas was merry and pleasant.

May it bring to every one the full realization of what it means to wish—A HAPPY NEW YEAR.

PALATKA (1870)
THE FANTASTICS

The small town of Palatka to the southwest of St. Augustine had a horseback parade, called The Fantastics, each Christmas. The stores would close around eleven o'clock in the morning, and the young men of the town would mount their horses and ride out to a pre-arranged rendezvous point, where they changed from street clothes to costumes of various descriptions. Then the "princes, dukes, knights, cowboys, indians, soldiers, and pirates" would parade back into town on their horses, down Lemon Street and then up and down all the main streets of town, to the great pleasure and enthusiasm of bystanders. The children in particular took great pleasure in seeing the Fantastics.

TALLAHASSEE (1874)
SPORTS MATCHES AND A PARADE

Among the morning Christmas celebrations in the state capital was one by the local African-Americans, who had foot races, wrestling matches, and a greasy-pole competition. Later in the day, twenty-five members of a group called the Fantasticals paraded down Main Street. A man sitting on a long-eared critter was followed by some fifty African-American children in an even line across the street, each carrying a ten-foot-long switch. Everyone seemed to have a good time. (*The Weekly Floridian*, December 29, 1874)

HYPOLUXO (1870s)
A POSSUM DINNER

Charles Pierce reported in his *Pioneer Life in Southeast Florida* (1970) how in the 1870s one of the early settlers invited his neighbors for a Christmas feast of possum, which he had fattened on sweet potatoes for over a month. The neighbors, who brought their Dutch oven with them to bake some biscuits, sailed over by boat the day before Christmas, carrying with them, as was customary in those days, bedding and mosquito bars to spend the night on the floor of their host's home. In fact, most people, even homeowners, slept on the floor since beds or cots were scarce at that time.

The next morning, Christmas Day, everyone woke up to a bright day and began making preparations for the big meal. The men started a large fire to obtain coals for the Dutch oven, and the host killed and prepared the possum. He placed sweet potatoes around the meat in the oven and covered it with thin strips of bacon. The meat took a long time to cook in the oven, but the guests didn't seem to mind as they stood around and discussed issues of the day. Captain Burnham, the keeper at Cape Canaveral Lighthouse, prepared a delicious cane syrup, something he had probably learned growing up in Vermont. Everyone had prickly pear pie for dessert.

In 1880, settlers in the area all gathered on Christmas Day for an outdoor picnic, something that fascinated newcomers from the North, who expected Christmas to be cold. Settlers traveled to Captain Dimick's hotel grounds, a site midway between settlements and therefore accessible to all. The cooks spent several days ahead of time preparing their specialties, whether main dishes, vegetables, or desserts. Willing hands assembled a long wooden table on sawhorses, the women placed their prized dishes all along its length, and everyone sat down for what turned out to be a sumptuous, hour-long feast.

Captain Dimick held a dance in his hotel after the meal, the first dance in the area, and had three local men provide musical accompaniment. That music inspired one young man to want to play the violin, an instrument he could buy at a small settlement near Jupiter Lighthouse for six dollars. To earn the money, he set about planting six thousand pineapple plants at one dollar per thousand at a local farm, a task that took him six long days to complete.

MIAMI (1874)
SEMINOLES CELEBRATE THE "WHITE MAN'S CHRISTMAS"

The Seminoles around Miami were invited to celebrate the "white man's Christmas" in 1874 at Brickell Point, the home of Miami's pioneer white family, the Brickells, who came to the area in 1871 and settled at the mouth of the Miami River. As described in the journal *Tequesta* (1980), the thirty Indians of all ages included Key West Billy, Billy Sunshine, Miami Doctor, Miami Jimmie, Cypress Tommie, Johnnie Jumper, Big Mouth Tiger, and Young Tiger Tail. With the women serving them and keeping the fires burning and pot boiling, the Indians ate their supper as they grouped around a kettle of *sof-kee*, a mix of coontie starch and green corn. The men shared one large wooden spoon that they dipped into the gruel heating in the large brass kettle. Other foods were alligator tail, terrapin, and garfish, as well as sweet potatoes and bananas. The men drank coffee and whiskey and reminisced about former Indians and adventures. The children played with rattles made from palmetto leaves woven together with shells inside. Then the Indians danced and smoked cigars.

When a rainstorm came up suddenly around midnight, the Indians used brush and palmetto leaves to make a strong shelter, under which everyone, Indians and whites alike, huddled. Two of the oldest men present, an Indian and an ex-Confederate soldier, were accorded places of honor and given many courtesies and much liquor. Eventually, "King Bourbon" overcame them both, and they fell asleep side by side "to sleep and dream of past battles."

When Christmas Day dawned, everyone had one final dance, after which the Indians invited the whites to attend the "Indian Christmas," their Green Corn Dance, in the future.

ST. AUGUSTINE (1876)
THE GREASY POLE

A file in the St. Augustine Historical Society contains a description of the Christmas games held in the city in 1876. After spectators had made their way down to the city wharf at the foot of Cathedral Street, they watched the yacht and canoe races, then the horse races from the yacht basin to the fort. Another sport consisted of horse riders jumping over a three-foot-high, moss-covered hurdle near the Spanish prison; to make matters more of a challenge, the riders carried an egg on a spoon and attempted to jump over the hurdle without breaking the egg.

The main attraction was a tall mast on one of the boats in the yacht basin. Four young men tried to climb the grease-coated pole, even resorting to climbing on top of each other's shoulders to reach the top of the mast, all of which caused much laughter from the spectators, especially when the climbers toppled down on one another. To help the climbers, someone provided a five-foot ladder, but even that did not get the men to the top of the pole.

Finally, some sailors from one of the boats told the climbers to get several three-foot-long pieces of rope and sticks to tie to the ends of the rope. Then a climber worked his way up the greasy pole, placing first one piece of rope around the pole and then the other, all the while pulling himself up very slowly. He made it to the top of the pole—to the great delight of the spectators, some appropriate music from the barracks band, and several loud blasts from a nearby cannon. For his efforts the winner received a ham that had been placed at the top of the pole and some money, all of which he shared with the other three climbers.

FERNANDINA (1878)
AN ORANGE TREE

The children from the local Methodist church decorated a holly tree with candles, toys, useful articles, and oranges so cleverly fastened to the tree that they seemed to have grown there. After a reading from the Scriptures, prayers, and songs, someone read the name of each child from a gift near the tree, at which point the child accepted the present with much glee. (*Florida Mirror*, December 28, 1878)

The same newspaper the previous week cautioned "mechanics and laboring men" to show self-restraint in spending money at Christmastime: "The man who lives in a rented house should take thought of the fact that the ten, twenty or fifty dollars which he may heedlessly spend for presents for his family would become the nucleus of a fund to be set aside for the purchase of a home for the wife and the little ones." (*Florida Mirror*, December 21, 1878)

GAINESVILLE (1880)
SHOPPING, PARADING, AND DANCING

According to the *Florida Mirror* out of Fernandina (January 1, 1881), the business streets of Gainesville were filled in the days before Christmas 1880 with throngs of shoppers "to supply the hundreds of Santa Claus[es] who would make thousands of happy souls on Christmas morning." Christmas itself saw the firing of many cannon and Chinese firecrackers to commemorate the day. Hens, which had been very stingy in supplying eggs the previous days, outdid themselves on Christmas morning to supply the large amount of eggnog made in the town.

Many African-Americans in town paraded through Gainesville on horseback, dressed in false faces and accompanying the local band, which played marches like "Dixie," "Yankee Doodle," and "Put Me in My Little Bed."

At the J. R. Beville Plantation that morning, the slaves went from their quarters up to the big house of the master for Christmas treats and presents. The procession of 160 African-Americans included the men in front, followed by the women and children, all accompanied by those who could play a musical instrument, whether fiddle, banjo, or tambourine. When they reached the master's house, the slaves marched three times around the house, "playing and singing praises to the master and mistress," who then served the men some drink and a plug of tobacco, the women some cakes and candies, and the children some toys.

That afternoon, Dr. Bacon gave a free magic show at Roper's Hall, although only the white children were allowed to attend. At night, he gave a similar performance for the older children and adults. He donated the admission fee to the fund for purchasing a children's library.

All made plans to attend an elegant New Year's ball and supper at the Arlington Hotel, which had served a sumptuous Christmas dinner, a meal that—with some exaggeration on the newspaper's part—"could hardly be equaled by Delmonico in New York City."

TAMPA (1882)
JOUSTING TOURNAMENT

In 1882, Tampa was a small town with fewer than a thousand inhabitants. To celebrate Christmas, the townsfolk, inspired by Sir Walter Scott's *Ivanhoe* and determined to preserve something from the "lost cause" of the Confederacy, reenacted the tilting formerly practiced in jousting tournaments. The young men would tilt for rings at Fort Brooke on the day after Christmas, then that evening attend a fancy costume ball, the principal social event of the year. Hundreds of people from the area trekked to Tampa for the festivities.

To prepare for the tournament, the young men, all of whom had to be at least sixteen years old and single, would spend many afternoons at the fort practicing their skills. Their practice would attract throngs of men and boys to the veranda of the long barracks building, where they would root for participants with names of historical or fictional knights such as Wilfred from *Ivanhoe* or the Knight of the Lost Cause.

On tournament day, each would-be knight, wearing a fancy dress uniform with a colorful sash, mounted his horse, carrying a lance that was at least eight feet long and tapered at the end. The young men raced toward the small rings suspended from a pole and plucked them as they rode by. All the participants were to act as chivalrously as possible toward others, especially those who were disqualified for falling off their horses or dropping their lances. The winner, who had the most rings on his lance, could crown his lady as the Queen of Love and Beauty, while the three runners-up could name their female companions, Maids of Honor. That evening, the winning knight and his Queen of Love and Beauty reigned over the ball.

Such tournaments continued into the early twentieth century. Tournament Street in Ft. Myers commemorates them, and other Florida cities, such as Daytona Beach and Tallahassee, had similar contests.

EUSTIS (1882)
CHRISTMAS WITHOUT SNOW

The following entry in C. R. Gilbert's diary for December 25, 1882, described a simple Christmas celebration in Eustis: "Christmas without snow, or frost, or chilly winds but we had Christmas all the same, and a Christmas tree too, at the Guller house. I was presented with a pipe, an apple from the cold north, some malted [?] candies, and a bottle marked parorgasic [?] for Dr. Gilbert. Well it was home like at least."

FERNANDINA (1884)
BLIND TOM

Blind Tom, the most famous black concert artist of the nineteenth century, gave a Christmas recital in Fernandina in 1884. Known officially as Thomas Greene Wiggins, Blind Tom traveled throughout America, astonishing crowds with his piano playing and showmanship: he could sing one song while playing a different one with his right hand and another one with his left hand. That Christmas season, he was part of Fernandina's holiday festivities, which included a large roller-skating carnival and ball.

The Methodist church, as was its custom, had a party in which the children (called "happy scholars") and their teachers were given gifts. After a program of songs, the officials of the church went to the holly tree, which was the center of the ceremony, clipped the presents from the tree, added fruit and bags of candies, and distributed them to the guests present. *The Florida Mirror* (December 27, 1884) noted that "the pastor seemed to be particularly fortunate, for it seemed that about every fourth or fifth name called was his."

The Mallory Line steamship that arrived in Fernandina at that time brought many Italian immigrants, who probably witnessed some of the local events before heading to south Florida to help build the railroads there. The same steamship then returned to New York carrying Florida cotton, oranges, cedar, rosin, and cans of shrimp. The immigrants would have seen on display in town a huge lemon newly brought from the Lake Panasoffkee area of central Florida: it measured twenty-four inches in circumference and weighed almost five pounds.

FORT MYERS (1885)
A BEEF SHOOT

As described by Karl Grismer in *The Story of Fort Myers* (1982), residents of Ft. Myers in 1885 began celebrating Christmas on December 24 with fireworks, followed the next morning by a "Beef Shoot," in which the best marksmen competed for a young steer, firing their rifles a hundred yards at a target. The five winners later divided the steer among themselves. A second contest was held the day after Christmas, with the prize, a pair of boots, going to the best shooter, but the poor shooting scores indicated that the riflemen had probably been celebrating too late the night before. What they had attended the night before, along with most of the area residents, was a Christmas party at the Keystone Hotel. There, the participants searched for eggs, which were then mixed up in a large bowl to make eggnog, whose potency was "equalled only by the kick of a very angry mule."

On the day after Christmas, according to Harnett Kane's *Southern Christmas Book* (1958), everyone turned out to see a cowboy tournament that resembled medieval English tournaments and replicas in Virginia, from which one of the residents came (see section on Tampa, 1882). To make it safer than the original tournaments, the contestants raced their horses across the field and aimed their lances, not at each other, but at three rings suspended in a line from horizontal bars ten feet off the ground. Each rider, who was given a name such as Knight of the Lost Cause, Knight of the Lone Star, or Knight of the White Plume, had three tries to pierce the rings. The best horsemen could pierce nine rings. The winner then chose his Queen of Love and Beauty who was crowned at a festival that evening along with a First and Second Maid of Honor. The tournament was held each Christmas until 1914, when World War I ended such festivities.

JACKSONVILLE (1890)
FIRECRACKERS

As happened in many Florida towns, revelers in Jacksonville in 1890 celebrated the birth of Jesus by blowing horns and lighting Chinese firecrackers. At least one editorial writer waged a campaign against such noise and hoped that authorities would enforce the statute that forbade the firing of firecrackers within city limits.

EUSTIS (1890)
CHURCH SERVICES

People in the small town of Eustis in central Florida celebrated Christmas with church services, including a sermon by the Reverend C. Grubb of St. Thomas (Episcopal) Church on the lives of missionaries among African children. The young boys in attendance, however, were more interested in a "fish pond" at the church, not one that contained real fish but one with tin horns, drums, and other presents the children could catch. The evening ended with lots of ice cream, cake, nuts, candy, and oranges. A reporter for Jacksonville's *Daily Florida Standard* noted that "the little folks seemed too small to contain the immense amount of happiness and ice cream offered them." Many locals planned on taking a steamboat excursion around Lakes Eustis and Harris to complete the holiday.

JACKSONVILLE (1891)
THE PERFORMANCE OF THE COUNT OF MONTE CRISTO

On Christmas Day 1891, famed actor James O'Neill performed at Jacksonville's Park Opera House in the lead role of *The Count of Monte Cristo*, which he had made famous all over America. On the day after Christmas, O'Neill presented for the first time in Jacksonville his drama entitled *The New South*. The fact that the opera house was filled, even though it was Christmas, was evidence that Floridians enjoyed seeing skilled, visiting performers, who no doubt were glad to take advantage of Florida's normally beautiful December weather.

CHIPLEY (1893)
NO FIGHT AT CHRISTMAS

The Chipley Banner reported on December 30, 1893, that the holidays passed without any fight to report.

CASSADAGA (1897)
SPIRITS COMMUNICATE

The Volusia County Record (January 1, 1898) reported that on Christmas Eve, many people went to the cottage of Mrs. Carrie Pratt, who entertained with music and recitations.

A Graphophone played instrumental music, songs, and orations, refreshments were served, and then "conditions were made and many from the spirit world through the mediumship of Mrs. Pratt came with their messages of love and greeting." Cassadaga, just south of DeLand, has long been famous for the many spiritualists—religious devotees who claim they can communicate with the spirit world—who live there.

Cassadaga has long attracted people deeply interested in the spiritual.
Florida State Archives

LEMON CITY (1890s)
CHRISTMAS PICNIC ON THE BEACH

The pioneer settlement of Lemon City on Biscayne Bay has long since disappeared, swallowed by the growing metropolis around it, but some descendants of the town's early settlers still live in the area. In the 1890s, the few families who lived there would get together to celebrate Christmas. As described in Thelma Peters' book *Lemon City: Pioneering on Biscayne Bay, 1850-1925* (1976), the families would cut their own Christmas tree from the nearby woods and decorate it with some store-bought balls and tinsel carefully preserved from year to year, as well as Spanish moss, wildflowers, palmettos, and palms. Other decorations included strings of popcorn, coontie berries, pinecones that the children painted with bright colors, and candy brought from Key West and Juno.

The families sometimes went by boat to the beach for a Christmas picnic. Some of the more enterprising formed the Alabama Troubadours, a blackface minstrel show that went from house to house, entertaining the appreciative audience and partaking in lemonade and cake along the way.

Santa would show up at some of the more public celebrations, wearing fake snowflakes and distributing presents such as dolls in the latest Parisian style, candy, nuts, raisins, and books for all the children. The youngsters would then recite prepared pieces and sing some well-practiced songs.

Christmas greeting in the Florida sand.
Florida State Archives

PENSACOLA (1897)
CHRISTMAS MENU

Mrs. Peter Olsen served the following dinner to her family and guests on Christmas Day 1897:

> Oysters on the Half Shell
> Celery Soup
> Roast Suckling Pig
> Peas
> Sweet Potatoes
> Creamed Potatoes
> Relishes
> Olives

Celery
Salted Almonds
Roast Turkey with Dressing
Cranberry Sauce
Salad
Pickled Peaches
Christmas Plum Pudding
Ice Cream
Fruit Cake
Mince Pie
Christmas Cake
Fruit
Neapolitan Cake
Nuts
Cocoanut Cake
Wines
Bon-Bons
Cheese
Black Coffee

Such a meal took much planning. Families actually began the preparations right after Thanksgiving. Cattle and hogs were butchered, smoked, and made into corned beef and sausage. Three days before Christmas, the cooks went into high gear, baking numerous cakes (pound, nut, coconut, chocolate, marble, jelly, and others). Some cooks made at least twenty pounds of fruitcake. On Christmas Eve, the turkey and chickens were butchered and prepared, and on Christmas Day, family and friends gathered to partake of the feast. Even strangers were welcome to help finish the food.

CHIPLEY (1899)
YULETIDE ADVICE

The Chipley Banner (December 23, 1899) had some "DONT'S FOR CHRISTMAS," which included the following:

Don't pay more for the Christmas tree than you pay for the fruit.

Don't send your gentleman adorer a gold toothpick. He may have false teeth.

Don't send your pastor embroidered slippers. To travel the

strait and narrow path requires hobnailed shoes.

Don't buy your daughter a piano and your wife a washtub. If you reverse the order, you will do justice to both.

Don't place your expectations of a Christmas gift too high. You may have to put your foot in your stocking to find anything in it.

Don't give your boy a drum and forbid him beating it, nor your daughter a horse and order her not to take it out of the stable without your permission.

ST. AUGUSTINE (1899)
SUNNY DAYS

According to the local *Tatler* newspaper, Christmas morning in 1899 was sunny and bright as throngs of people filled the plaza on their way to different churches. Catholics, for example, could attend one of three masses in the Cathedral, beginning at six o'clock in the morning and ending with a special Vespers service in the evening. The tall, stately edifice was full of decorations, and the altar inside had many candles. Trinity Church was also filled with Christmas greens, and special music for the occasion was sung for the worshippers.

The Alcazar Hotel (now the Lightner Museum) had ropes of spruce, garlands of wild ivy and holly, and a large Christmas tree with many incandescent lights gleaming for all the guests. Each table in the dining room had red containers full of holly. Each breakfast guest received a cornucopia of Christmas sweets; in the evening, each diner received a large slice of fruitcake in a pretty box in addition to dessert. Menus of the lavish dinner (called a "Lucullian feast") were enclosed in an artistic cover, which diners could take home as souvenirs.

The highlight of the day for many of the local children was the distribution of presents in the hotel at four o'clock. With a flourish of horns and other types of music, Santa Claus entered the decorated room from the chimney, shook hands with all of those who claimed they had been good that year, and distributed toys for the children and appropriate presents for the adults, including one brass cannon filled with sweets. Among the featured guests who arrived by train were composer John Philip Sousa and his wife.

The soldiers at St. Francis Barracks had a huge Christmas dinner of soup, roasts, vegetables, celery, three kinds of pie, plum pudding, nuts, fruit, cheese, coffee, and lager beer. Even the prisoners at Fort Marion had turkey, vegetables, pies, and puddings, as well as the chance to smoke some tobacco.

The less fortunate of the town received help from the King's Daughters and Relief Society, as well as from a special fund raised by the *Evening Record* newspaper. Everyone seems to have celebrated the day in pleasant fashion.

Today, the Lightner Museum often recreates a Victorian Christmas during December.

PENSACOLA (1901)
FOOTBALL, RABBIT CHASE, AND FIRECRACKERS

Christmas Day 1901 in Pensacola saw a wide variety of activities. A football match was to pit the local Barrancas Eleven against a college team from Auburn, Alabama, but, when the college team pulled out the day before the game, the officer in charge of the game convinced the Montgomery (Alabama) Athletic Club to play the local Pensacola soldiers. The game was played at the newly renovated Palmetto Beach, which boasted a new circular racetrack, a football/baseball field built inside the racetrack, and a large grandstand with three strings of barbed wire placed between the spectators and the playing field (to discourage people from running onto the field). The locals were pleased when their team beat the visitors, 5-0.

For the rabbit chase, six dogs were released to chase a rabbit around the playing field. The rabbit eventually found a hole in the surrounding wall and escaped—much to the delight of many in the crowd. The manager of the field announced that at least five rabbit chases would be held on the field the following week.

To the dismay of many, Mayor Jones lifted the ban on the discharge of fireworks within city limits from December 24 until January 2, 1902. Many local boys then proceeded to shoot off fireworks until the early hours of Christmas Day itself, much to the annoyance of those trying to sleep. After catching a few hours of sleep themselves, the boys resumed their noisemaking throughout Christmas Day, disrupting the religious services in various churches. For those citizens who dreaded the pandemonium caused by the firecrackers during that week, they had to look forward to the same situation in the upcoming February carnival.

PENSACOLA (1902)
NEWSPAPER CARRIERS ASK FOR CHRISTMAS TIPS

Pensacola's *Daily News* (December 26, 1902) printed a holiday poem asking for tips for the newspaper boys:

THE DAILY NEWS 1902 CARRIERS' ADDRESS

> Merry Christmas to you, mister!
> Do you think that you'd enjoy
> All them good things, when you've missed a
> Present for your carrier boy?
>
> When you light your Christmas taper,
> An' the day is growin' dim,
> An' you're kickin' 'bout your paper,
> Don't you ever think of him—
>
> Him what brings it when he'd ruther
> Be at home, where other boys is—
> Him that p'raps ain't got no mother,
> An' don't know what Christmas toys is?
>
> If you don't, I think you orter;
> Christmas comes but once a year,
> An' I'm waiting on you, sorter
> Anxious as it's drawin' near.
>
> I don't want no toys nor candy—
> No, nor books nor good advice;
> But there's things what comes in handy
> When a feller's got the price.
>
> Some folks say my route's a poor one—
> That my patrons ain't no good;
> But I think that it's a sure one,
> So I'm just "a-sawin' wood."
>
> Ain't a-sayin' much—jest waitin'
> On you people still, because
> 'Tain't no use a-calculatin'
> On them tales of Santa Claus.

All the Santa Claus I know is
Them what lives along my route;
An' I know my only show is
In my patrons shellin' out.

This ain't beggin'—all good people,
Kinder opens up to boys,
When they hears from yonder steeple
Christmas chimes sound Christmas joys.
Christ, they say, was born on Christmas,
I dunno—I know I'm livin';
An' it sorter seems if I was
Big as you, I'd feel like givin'.

ST. MARKS LIGHTHOUSE (EARLY 1900s)
ISOLATION ON THE COAST

The isolation of lighthouses around Florida made living in them difficult and lonely. Lighthouse families had to become self-sufficient for entertainment and education. One lighthouse family, the Greshams, who took care of St. Marks Lighthouse from 1892 until 1957, had a very private life since their site was accessible only by boat (much later by seaplane and car). At Christmastime in the early 1900s, the children there would receive gifts from the Ringling family of Sarasota and hunters from Pensacola, all of whom had partaken of the hospitality of the lighthouse keeper's family on hunting trips.

PENSACOLA (EARLY 1900s)
CHURCH SERVICES

Christmas celebrations in Pensacola revolved around church services. Pensacolians placed cribs in the different churches. At midnight on Christmas Eve, an image of the Christ child was placed in each crib. Midnight Mass was celebrated in the Catholic churches to the accompaniment of the ringing of the church bells.

At Christ Church, during Christmas Eve services, all the lights were extinguished at midnight, but hundreds of candles burned brightly. The Junior Choir and congregation joined in softly singing "Silent Night, Holy Night," which helped everyone think about the true meaning of the season.

PALATKA (1912)
CHRISTMAS TURKEY ATTACKS EX-SENATOR

Ex-state senator S. J. Hilburn was attacked by a wild turkey in the back-yard of his home in Palatka in 1912 and sustained some serious injuries that might have been life-threatening. He was about to kill a turkey hen chosen for the Christmas meal when, all of a sudden, a wild turkey that had come out of the woods to take up with the tame bird attacked the man. The angry turkey leaped into the air and attacked Hilburn with out-stretched legs and sharp claws and spurs. He scratched Hilburn's face, split open his hand, and was about to attack his eyes when the politician grabbed a gun and did the sixteen-pound bird in. The shaken politician declared in the local newspaper that the Congressional bout he had had with one Frank Clark several months before paled into "utter insignificance when compared with the encounter he had with the enraged turkey gobbler."

JACKSONVILLE (1912)
THE ST. NICHOLAS GIRL

Jacksonville had suffered through a hard autumn in 1912: smallpox had driven people inside; soldiers with fixed bayonets had patrolled the city until Thanksgiving after a streetcar strike had turned violent; and merchants were suffering a poor season. Instead of Santa Claus that December, *The Florida Times-Union* had the St. Nicholas Girl take his place. Perky and pretty in her Santa Claus hat and a red suit with furry white trim and black boots, the St. Nicholas Girl accepted letters from children and had Santa's sleigh filled with presents by the time it arrived at the Morocco Temple of the Shrine on Christmas morning. She encouraged the children to ask for what they really wanted, not so much what they needed.

MIAMI (1917)
WORLD WAR I CURTAILS CHRISTMAS

During World War I, residents of Miami, like most citizens of the United States, usually had meatless meals on Tuesdays in order to observe the conservation movement that limited lavish meals during wartime. When Christmas 1917 fell on a Tuesday, the managers of Miami hotels and restaurants agreed to observe the meatless custom and not serve pork, beef, or mutton, although they were allowed to serve fish and fowl.

Because of the stringent war conditions, Christmas celebrations in Miami Sunday schools did not include the giving of candies and other gifts customary during the holidays. Instead, the money that would have been spent on such niceties was given to charities such as orphanages and Armenian relief agencies.

The Miami Herald (December 25, 1917) reminded readers how the weather was elsewhere:

> If the weather man's promise holds good, Christmas will dawn in Miami with the skies partly overcast with clouds and the weather warm, while a large part of the country is wrapt in a sheet of snow and ice and chilled by the breath of a howling blizzard which is sweeping down from the northwest carrying with it temperatures of ten to twenty-five degrees below zero in some sections of the northwest.

The paper reveled in the fact that many in south Florida would "conclude the day's festivities in the well-established Miami way—a swim in the surf."

SEBASTIAN (1920s)
SIMPLE CHRISTMASES

In *More Tales of Sebastian* (1992), long-time residents told about early Christmas traditions in that part of southeastern Florida. Stockings would usually hold items such as candy, card games, a harmonica, jacks, marbles, and nuts. A particular treat was a large metal pail full of hard candies that would last throughout the year or a beautiful doll with a china head. The local school would put on a program for the families and have a tree with a small gift for each child. The children would sing carols, often somewhat out of tune. Families would also cut their own trees, a large one for the living room and a smaller one for the children's room.

One family planted a small native holly tree at the southeast corner of Main Street and Central Avenue. For years the family tended the tree, but didn't add lights until the mid-1930s, when it had grown tall. When the tree grew too tall for someone to put the handmade star on top with a stepladder, a man had to bring in a wrecker to reach the top of the branches. The tree was finally taken down to make room for what became the Teen Center.

HIALEAH (1923)
A CHRISTMAS PLAY SET IN FLORIDA

In a Christmas play in the community church, all 135 children enrolled in the local school appeared in "A Visit to Santa Claus' House." The four-act play, as described in *The Miami Herald* (December 23, 1923), first shows a mother and daughter discussing the lack of school funds and their difficulty in arranging some school entertainment because they have no auditorium, piano, Victrola, or anything else with which to work. In act two, the mother dreams about angels, fairies, brownies, Santa, and all his workmen on their way to Hialeah to save the day by having the children go to Santa's house. In the last two acts, the mother and daughter go to the house, which they find is made of magic bricks instead of snow and ice. Santa then presents each child with a "magic brick," which turns out to be a box of candy. Such plays that made a Florida setting a prominent part of the action probably made the celebration of the holiday all the more meaningful to the children.

DAYTONA (1925)
PROHIBITION HOOCH WASHES ASHORE

The Yuletide season was unexpectedly made much brighter, or at least wetter, for many coastal residents near Daytona when hundreds—possibly thousands—of boxes of contraband whiskey washed ashore from a two-masted schooner, *Fulshem*, which sank in a strong winter storm at

Christmas 1925. For weeks afterwards, beachgoers scanned the horizon for some telltale sign that another box of whiskey was making its way towards shore.

Five crew members and an inexperienced captain making his first trip went down with the ship.

A 1920s Florida Christmas. Note the orange tree decorated with Christmas cards.
Florida State Archives

When the body of young Captain Hudson washed up on the beach, along with many cases of whiskey from the sunken schooner, searchers discovered that the young man had been named captain of the boat just two hours before it sailed. The young newlywed had planned to earn enough money so he and his new bride could settle in Nova Scotia, but the weather gods had other plans for him, plans that made his first trip his last.

Remnants of that whiskey cargo came ashore for weeks after the sinking, but no records indicate that the finders turned in the crates to local authorities.

KEY LARGO (1925)
CHRISTMAS AND A WEDDING ANNIVERSARY

The residents of the Florida Keys in the early part of this century suffered hardships that included deprivation and scarcity of goods. As described by Jerry Wilkinson in *Florida Keys Magazine* (December 1994), Alice Shaw kept a diary, beginning in 1925, after she and her family arrived from Mississippi.

> [December 8:] I do not like this place because of the strangeness, the pests, and inconveniences. . . . so little available water I have to be stingy with it. There is no place indoors for washing and the rocky ground and distracting mosquitoes and sand flies make it awful trying to wash outdoors. I have only three tiny tubs, no conveniences, and a two-week's washing for five people. I hate to complain, but my mind is a tumult of discontented complaint.
>
> [December 23:] There are no picture shows, libraries, schools or churches here; nothing but post-office, [train] station, a very limited country store; and the 'hotel' by courtesy so called. After dinner came the Christmas program and going after the little tree for ourselves[:] a small, glossy leaved mangrove. We are to have a tropical Christmas and make our desserts from Key Largo tropical fruits. . . . Tomorrow is Christmas Eve. We shall have holiday and will toil and bake, clean and iron—if the oil stove will behave itself and grant permission. I hope this cold spell annihilates all the mosquitoes.
>
> [December 24:] This is Christmas Eve. The stove did

nicely, and I got all my Christmas baking done. Tonight, we went to the hotel for the Christmas tree entertainment. After distribution of the small gifts and confections, there was fun, sleight of hand, tricks, and singing all of the many beautiful favorites until midnight. When we came home, Everitt and I played Santa Claus together for the little folks as we have done so many years.

[December 25:] Christmas Day and our 16th anniversary. The little folks were up before daylight, rejoicing in their new acquisitions. In the afternoon, they went swimming and rowing, and I played the violin. Then I put on my wedding dress and slippers for a little while and cut our anniversary cake when all my little family arrived. It is marked 16 this time. How time flies!

KEY LARGO (1926)
BEAUTIFUL WEATHER AND SANTA IN A BOAT

The following year, Alice Shaw had another beautiful holiday to remark on:

[December 25:] Christmas Day and such a lovely one. It is just like a June day, mild, warm, sunny and breezy[,] just perfect. Just like Lowell's lines: 'Oh, what is so rare as a day in June? Then, if ever, come perfect days.' We had oleanders, rose-colored and daintily fragrant in our vase and oranges from the island on our table, though oranges and limes are so scarce because of the storm-destroyed citrus groves.

When I got home, I fixed up a quick dinner and got the house in readiness for our guests, who came and spent several hours. We had fun, games, the graphophone, ice cream and cake and a general good time. Then Mr. Bruce, Mr. Carrish, Everitt and Junior had a pleasant motorride on the sound. After all left, I did not put on my wedding dress as I did last year, for the storm harmed my dress and ruined my slippers. I looked at the wedding clothes and wedding pictures and let the sweet memories of the happy past drift over me.

[December 26:] This morning, before Sunday School,

Key Largo had a most unique experience of gay, high adventure and delight, when Santa Claus, sent by the loving thought of the Junior Red Cross, came gliding into port in the dainty cruiser, 'Old Timer,' owned by Commodore Stephen C. Singleton and loaned to Santa Claus for his work of bringing joy—bestowing gifts to the bright little children of storm-ravaged Key Largo.

MIAMI (1926)
THE SEMINOLES CELEBRATE CHRISTMAS

At Christmas 1926, some local whites in Miami invited the local Seminoles to celebrate the holiday with them at Musa Isle, N.W. Twenty-seventh Avenue and Seventeenth Street, in an Indian village. Santa Claus himself showed up and led the Indians in a traditional Sun Dance, the tribal ritual of appreciation that goes around and around a tree. The organizers of the event, Mr. and Mrs. Lasher, spread the word throughout the Everglades, and many Seminoles showed up, partly out of curiosity about the white man's celebration. Equipped with alligator skins, food, and trappings for a stay of several days, the Indians came by any means available. After the Sun Dance, the Indians did their Snake Dance and then received gifts from Santa Claus, Mrs. Lasher, and Tony Tommy (the high chief of the Seminoles). The Lashers made arrangements to supply gifts to those Seminoles who had not been able to attend the festivities. The best gift went to Cory Osceola, an interpreter at the Indian village of Musa Isle: a brand-new Ford touring car painted green and decorated with red stripes.

Santa brings presents to Seminole children.
Florida State Archives

OCALA SCRUB (1928)
CRACKER FLORIDIANS CELEBRATE CHRISTMAS

When Marjorie Kinnan Rawlings moved to Cross Creek in 1928, she and her then-husband, Charles Rawlings, tried to raise oranges while they worked on their writing. In her well-received non-fiction work, *Cross Creek* (1942), she described Christmas at the Creek. Once, when she cooked turkey, squash, potatoes, and plum pudding, two men showed up to visit. Thinking that an invitation to dinner ("Dinner is ready. Won't you men join us?") would be a hint for them to leave, as it would be in the North where Rawlings grew up, she was quite surprised that the men agreed to stay, especially because the two uninvited guests had already eaten dinner. Believing that to refuse such an invitation was impolite, the men stayed and everyone was quite unhappy: Rawlings because her delayed dinner was dry, the men because they were full from their earlier meal. Taking great pride in what she called a "typical Yankee Christmas dinner," Rawlings made the mistake of asking the two men what a typical Cracker Christmas dinner was. "Whatever we can git, Ma'am," one of them responded to the greatly embarrassed Rawlings.

In Chapter 21, "Winter," of *Cross Creek*, Rawlings explained that Christmastime was busy at the Creek because that was the peak of the orange season, which demanded long hours picking, washing, grading, wrapping, and packing the fruit for shipment north. For various reasons (preoccupation with the oranges, poverty, tradition), Creek residents celebrated Christmas quietly. Mrs. Rawlings herself gave boxes of clothes, candy, and fruitcake to her African-American acquaintances and other neighbors, but none of them usually gave presents in return at the time. Instead, during the year they would give her gifts of wild grapes or blackberries, quail, or bass. One man studied hard about what to give her that she couldn't buy, then fixed his outboard motor, borrowed other boats from friends, set up duck blinds, and took out her party for a splendid duck hunt. As she wrote, "A millionaire could not have given a finer present."

FLORIDA KEYS (1940s)
CHURCH, STOPPER TREES, AND FOOD

Life on the Florida Keys was isolated from the rest of Florida until Henry Flagler's railroad to Key West connected the keys to the mainland in 1912. After a hurricane washed away much of that railroad in 1935, the federal government bought the right of way and constructed US Highway

1, which joined Key West to the mainland for good.

Growing up in the Keys had its advantages (good fishing, boating, and swimming) and disadvantages (lack of a lot of friends, few books, and few jobs), but Christmastime was still a special time. Presents were usually scarce, but at least everyone received some new clothes. The day itself often centered around a church service, especially if Christmas fell on a Sunday. In the Upper Keys, many residents went to the Methodist church, whereas in Key West most went to the Catholic church. Carols were sung at church and at home.

The main meal on the big day often included a turkey, which the residents had probably obtained from Key West and had kept penned outside. If a family had two turkeys, they would have one on Thanksgiving and one on Christmas. There might also be chicken, a ham (many families raised hogs), lots of vegetables, and a queen-of-all pudding: a custard pudding with a middle layer of guava jelly and a meringue top. The dessert could also be a sweet-potato pie or guava duff, a type of steamed cake topped with a sweet sauce. In Key West, the many workers in the cigar industry would have preferred a more Hispanic meal, including *lechon asado* (roast pork), *congris* (black beans and rice), boiled yucca, Spanish wine, and Spanish nougat.

Most people placed a Spanish stopper tree in their houses, perhaps decorated with seashells, handmade decorations, and even light bulbs found along the shore. To paint the tree, they mixed the juice of the prickly pear with bluing, berry juices, and other products. They secured small candles to the tree with two-pronged clothespins. Before electricity arrived in the 1940s, such candles served as tree lights.

During World War II, naval personnel stationed in Key West celebrated Christmas with religious services, pageants, boxing matches, and parties for the children. In 1943, some of them put on a play, "The Christmas Story," with forty singers from the ranks of the Waves, or Women Accepted for Volunteer Emergency Services, and enlisted men. Servicemen and -women of all faiths were invited to the chief Catholic service of the season. The day after Christmas was highlighted with a rendition of Handel's "Messiah" by one hundred civilians and Navy personnel. Such festivities allowed the servicemen and women, who were far away from home, some respite from a war that was taking its toll on ships off the Florida Keys. The beautiful setting and balmy weather would later lure many of the enlisted men back to the Keys and other parts of Florida with their families.

MIMS (1951)
TRAGEDY STRIKES A CIVIL RIGHTS LEADER

On Christmas Day 1951, an unknown assailant detonated a bomb under the house where civil rights leader Harry Tyson Moore and his wife were gathered with family members to celebrate the holiday. Moore and his wife, Harriette, held a family reunion that December to celebrate their wedding anniversary and the holiday. After everyone retired for the night, the bomb went off, destroying the house and fatally injuring Moore and his wife.

Many believed that the Ku Klux Klan had detonated the bomb, but no one was ever convicted of the crime. As the executive secretary of the Florida branches of the National Association for the Advancement of Colored People (NAACP), Harry Moore was heavily involved in registering African-Americans to vote and working for equality for minorities. He was the first NAACP official to die because of his office, but he would not be the last. Today, the Harry T. Moore Center in Cocoa, Florida, honors this American hero.

TAMPA (1960s)
CUBAN CHRISTMASES

The thousands of Cuban immigrants to Florida have brought many customs from their homeland, including those associated with

Christmas. As described by Leland Hawes in *The Tampa Tribune* (December 24, 1983), one of those immigrants, Marcelino Oliva, brought the traditional *Noche Buena* observance to Tampa in 1943 and expanded it to include as many as four hundred friends by the 1960s. Two days before Christmas, Marcelino would take his grandsons to pick up the pigs he had butchered and cleaned. From a farm near Bushnell he had picked out the pigs, each of which weighed between thirty

Tampa at Christmas in the early 60s
Florida State Archives

and forty pounds. Those who did the cooking on Christmas Eve would marinate the meat overnight in a sauce of sour oranges, oregano, onion, and lots of garlic. The men would cover the pork with palm fronds and cook it for six or seven hours. Meanwhile, the women of the family prepared black beans, rice, salad, yucca, Cuban bread, and wine. For dessert they served *turon*, a Spanish nugget candy made with nuts.

When the guests arrived, they would hear recorded mariachi music. After the hearty meal, many would dance while others played bongo drums, maracas, and other instruments. Late in the evening, someone would give a speech, usually about the Cuban homeland in happier days, and before midnight everyone would go off to Mass.

JACKSONVILLE (1992)
CHRISTMAS POEM INSTEAD OF A PARKING TICKET

Shoppers returning to their cars around Christmas 1992 were pleasantly surprised to find that, although the time on the parking meter may have expired, they received an orange slip of paper with the following poem on their windshields instead of a citation:

'Tis the week before Christmas and all thru the city

People are shopping; so we will take pity.

No tickets today—We will not cite.

Merry Christmas to all and to all a good night.

Such a custom, repeated in many towns, represented the leniency shown by the police toward minor lawbreakers, reflecting the very old practice of allowing debtors to skip a payment due on Christmas Day.

RAIFORD (1997)
DEATH ROW INMATES MINGLE WITH THE CLERGY

As has happened every Christmas for twenty years, inmates on Death Row met with volunteer clergy for a change of pace from their routine. Fourteen inmates at a time filed into a room for a twenty-minute respite of quiet Christmas music and a specially prepared meal of fried chicken, vegetables, and snacks. The Union Correctional Institution allowed volunteer ministers to talk to the inmates about life in prison, religion, or whatever came up.

No one had party hats or false hopes of release from their death sentences. Someone took a photograph of the inmates to send to their families. The three hundred condemned prisoners appreciated the effort by the Chaplaincy Services Holiday Project. One of the men said, "When you spend so much time in a place like this, you lose what the holiday is all about. It helps put that feeling back inside you, knowing somebody cares. I feel that these are my friends." The yearly session is the only social setting for the men besides weekend visits with family or private meetings with ministers.

The superintendent of the prison, Dennis O'Neill, explained his motives behind allowing the ministers their Christmas visit: "No matter what the depths are to which they [the inmates] have descended criminally, I think it still helps to be humane."

This practice is reminiscent of many such Christmas traditions in Florida. For example, prisoners in the Dade County Jail back in 1923 received presents from family, friends, and the Salvation Army, and the sheriff had a special meal served, of which everyone could have two or more helpings if he so desired. Cigars and cigarettes were also distributed to the inmates.

ETHNIC CELEBRATIONS IN FLORIDA

Among its fifteen million residents, Florida has a rich heritage of ethnic groups, people who may speak other languages, eat different foods, and celebrate holidays in unique ways. Many different peoples who have come here from other countries or states have brought with them the traditions, customs, and foods associated with their former homes and/or ethnic groups. While one can argue that the longer the immigrants remain in Florida, the more Americanized they become, one can also see how most ethnic communities, especially those with a sizable number of like-minded individuals, retain their particular characteristics. I have described here ten of the larger groups to symbolize the many people who have come from different places. I have included one recipe associated with each group that is served at Christmastime. Many of these dishes hearken back to the Old World and have been handed down from generation to generation. They are prepared just once a year and can be made with readily available ingredients.

AFRICAN-AMERICANS

Many African-Americans throughout the United States as well as Florida, which has the fourth largest African-American population in this country, celebrate the nonreligious festival of *Kwanzaa* from December 26 to January 1. Established in 1966 by Maulana Karenga, chairman of Black Studies and director of the African-American Cultural Center at California State University, Long Beach, it has become a time of cultural reaffirmation and a celebration of family and social values. The festival took its name from the Swahili word *kwanza*, meaning "first"—as in the phrase *matunda ya kwanza* ("first fruits")—with the additional "a" distinguishing the African-American celebration from the African one.

During *Kwanzaa's* time of fasting, feasting, and self-examination, participants observe seven nights of reflection and try to avoid the commercialization so prevalent at Christmastime. *Kwanzaa,* based on African harvest festivals, emphasizes seven principles: *umoja* (unity), *kujichagulia* (self-determination), *ujima* (collective work and responsibility), *ujamaa* (cooperative economics), *Nia* (purpose), *kuumba* (creativity), and *imani* (faith).

Participants discuss each of the principles on separate evenings of the celebration after they light a candle in the *kinara,* the seven-branched candleholder that holds black, red, and green candles symbolizing the seven principles of African-American family life. Family members exchange gifts during the celebration, especially handmade items and small tokens

African-Americans celebrated Christmas in the 1940s with fellowship and the giving of presents.
Florida State Archives

of appreciation. They then partake of a family meal, which may include Romaine Salad.

When a family celebrates *Kwanzaa* at home, the mother sets the ceremonial table and places on it an ear of corn to symbolize each of her children. A decorated unity cup, called *kikombe,* is used each evening to make toasts. On December 31, the family may join other families for a feast called the *karamu.*

ROMAINE SALAD WITH ORANGE AND RADISH
2 small heads of romaine lettuce
1 bunch of radishes
3 large navel oranges
1 ½ tbs. of red wine vinegar
5 tbs. of olive oil

Wash the lettuce, cut it into bite-size pieces, and place it in a large salad bowl. Wash the radishes, slice them into pieces, and add to the bowl. Peel each orange, separating the peel from the inner membrane with a sharp knife. Add the orange pieces to the bowl. Squeeze the orange pulp into the bowl to retain as much of the juice as possible. Prepare a vinaigrette with the remaining ingredients, including one tablespoon of the squeezed orange juice. Grate some of the larger radish pieces over the salad and gently pour the dressing over the salad. Serve at once.

CZECHS

Florida has several communities of Czechs, especially in south Florida and in Hernando County in the small town of Masaryktown. Those who celebrate the "old-fashioned" way pay special attention to Christmas Eve, especially the meal on that evening.

Those who follow Czech customs begin the Christmas season on St. Nicholas Day (*Svaty Mikulas*), December 6. St. Nicholas, a former bishop in Europe, is believed to descend from heaven on that day on a golden cord, accompanied by a white-clothed angel and a black-clothed devil, called *Cert* who has a whip and chain to threaten children who have misbehaved. Before going to bed on December 5, Czech children place dishes on a table, hoping that St. Nicholas will fill the dishes with candies and other goodies during the night.

On December 6, families have an acquaintance or an older child dress up as St. Nicholas and lead a black-dressed "devil" with a large chain to the door of each house. St. Nicholas then questions the children to see how well they know their prayers and, after thoroughly frightening the youngsters and maybe even examining a large book listing the names of all good children, distributes treats (apples, candy, gingerbread, and nuts) and gifts to them. St. Nicholas, in return, receives small presents from the parents.

The Christmas Eve meal—often preceded by a day of fasting or a day when fried carp, potato salad, and vanilla crescent cookies are served— begins when someone, often a grandmother or mother, walks into the dining room holding a lit candle. Each person around the table receives *oplatky,* a very thin white wafer imprinted with the image of Jesus and Mary. The celebrants then dip the wafer into a container of honey and eat it to ward off death, although some of the more superstitious save part of the wafer for continued protection. Then everyone sings Slovak hymns, and someone reads from a prayer book.

Next follows the walnut ceremony, in which each person cracks a walnut and looks inside, hoping to find a shell with no nut inside, which means a successful year ahead. The main meal, which includes sausage, rice, kielbasa, sauerkraut, and plum soup, is served. Roast duck and dumplings may be substituted for some of the main ingredients. Then follows poppy-seed buns dipped in milk and butter. After the meal, everyone goes to the midnight church service.

Christmas Day itself is usually a quiet time when people visit relatives, wishing each other *"Prejeme Vam Vesele Vanoce a stastny Novy Rok"* ("Merry Christmas"). The holidays continue through St. Stephen's Day (December 26), New Year's Eve, and *Tri Kralu,* the Evening of Three Kings (January 6), at which time the Czechs take down their Christmas tree.

VANILKOVE ROHLICKY (VANILLA CRESCENTS)
½ lb. unsalted, softened butter
½ cup sugar
2 cups sifted all-purpose flour
1¼ cups ground unblanched almonds
½ tsp. salt
1 tsp vanilla extract
Confectioners' sugar

Cream the butter and sugar together with an electric mixer at medium speed until light and fluffy. Mix in the flour ½ cup at a time, then add almonds, vanilla extract, and salt. Continue to beat mixture until it becomes a slightly stiff dough. Shape the dough into a ball, wrap in wax paper, and place in the refrigerator for one hour.

Preheat oven to 350°. Lightly butter two large baking sheets. Cut off small pieces of chilled dough and place them on a floured board. Roll each piece into a strip 1" wide and ½" thick, then form into the shape of a crescent. Place the crescents at least ½" apart on baking sheet. Bake in oven for 15–20 minutes, remove, and let cool for 5 minutes before transferring to a cake rack. Dust with confectioners' sugar. Makes 36 crescents.

FINNS

Florida's Palm Beach County has the largest Finnish-American community outside of Europe. Its thirty thousand Finnish-Americans and Finnish nationals are an important part of the economic and cultural activities of the area, especially in the cities of Lake Worth and Lantana. From as far back as 1906, Finns have been migrating to the area and have established churches, restaurants, clubs, and businesses. The annual Finnish-American heritage festival, Finlandia Days, held in Lake Worth's Bryant Park since 1985, features crafts and ethnic food as well as local and international entertainment.

The tightly knit community of Florida Finns tries to celebrate Christmas as closely as possible to the way their relatives do it in Finland. The time of year is important to Finns since it marks the winter solstice, when the days start to become longer and brighter. The three most important days of the Christmas holiday are Christmas Eve, Christmas Day, and New Year's Day.

The Finns, in fact, spend several weeks preparing for the holidays, beginning with musical renditions of Vogler's "Hosanna" on the first Sunday in Advent and proceeding with get-togethers, called *Pikkujoulu* (Little Christmas), to make Christmas decorations and enjoy each other's company in programs of music, talks, and good food. Family members who live far away try to return to celebrate the holidays with their extended families.

Unlike in Finland, where the Finns put up their Christmas trees on the last Sunday before Christmas, Florida Finns put theirs up much earlier, probably to extend the holiday season and make it more compatible with the way other Americans observe the season. They decorate their trees with rows of national flags as a symbol of friendship with other peoples.

On Christmas Eve, Finns eat the main meal of the holiday, which often includes rutabaga casserole, open their presents, and try to take part in the "Peace of Christmas" celebration in Lake Worth's Bryant Park. They may also place candles or wreaths on the graves of loved ones in local cemeteries.

When it comes time to distribute presents on Christmas Eve, many families hire a Finnish *Joulupukki* (Father Christmas) to do so. The local Finnish newspaper, *Amerikan Uutiset,* has an advertisement for the *Joulupukki,* or sometimes a family member plays the part. The children, dressed as Father Christmas' little helpers with caps and red tights, always answer "yes" when Father Christmas asks them, "Are there any good children here?" Father Christmas then distributes presents from a big basket, and the children sing to him.

On Christmas morning, Finnish churches in Florida are packed, since church services play an important part in the Finnish celebration. The centerpiece of the celebration, however, is the family, all of whom wish each other *"Hyvaa joulua"* ("Merry Christmas").

On New Year's Eve, friends often gather together with their children. Around midnight, the children light fireworks to bring in the New Year with as much noise as is allowed. The families may go to Finnish halls for dancing on New Year's Day.

RUTABAGA CASSEROLE

2 large rutabagas
1½ cups of cream or mixture of cream and milk
¾ cup of dried breadcrumbs
⅓ of a cup of dark syrup
1 egg, beaten
½ tsp. of white pepper
1½ tsp. of ground ginger
½ tsp. of grated nutmeg
1 tbs. of salt
Dried breadcrumbs
Butter

Preheat oven to 350°. Scrub and peel the rutabagas, cut into large pieces, and boil in lightly salted water until soft, about 30–40 minutes. Strain and set aside the cooking liquid. Mash or blend the rutabagas in a blender. Mix in the cream, dried breadcrumbs, dark syrup, beaten egg, spices, and the cooking liquid. Put mixture into a greased baking dish. Press the surface with a fork to make a pattern. Sprinkle a thick coating of dried breadcrumbs over casserole and drop pats of butter on top in small amounts. Bake for 2 hours.

GERMANS

Florida has attracted many visitors, especially during the cold European winters. The availability of direct flights to Florida has drawn countless Germans to visit and, in many cases, to move permanently to the Sunshine State.

Advent in Germany is an important season leading up to Christmas. German families, both in Europe and in Florida, may have an Advent wreath and will say a prayer before lighting it. Another tradition is to have a chocolate treat for each day during Advent leading up to Christmas. St. Nicholas Day, celebrated on December 6, is an important celebration for children, who, to honor the saint revered for his kindness, will put out their stockings or shoes for candies. Another favorite activity among children is to open another "door" on special Christmas cards each day.

Christmas celebrations usually begin on Christmas Eve, when many German families spend the evening at church services, wishing each other *"Froehliche Weihnachten"* ("Merry Christmas"). The Christ Child, rather than Santa Claus, brings presents on Christmas Eve. Some people light the candles on the Christmas tree right after the church service. Then families open their presents. Some German families in Florida have two Christmases: a German one on Christmas Eve, an occasion when they speak German all evening and open presents from their German relatives; and a more American Christmas, when they speak English and follow American customs. One of the favorite meals for Germans is stuffed breast of veal.

STUFFED BREAST OF VEAL
3 lbs. of veal with a pocket

1 tbs. lemon juice
½ tsp. pepper
½ loaf egg bread, cut into chunks
½ cup chopped onions
½ cup chopped ham or ground beef
½ cup chopped parsley
1 tbs. shortening
2 eggs, slightly beaten
¼ pound sausage
1 tsp. salt

Preheat oven to 500°. Sprinkle lemon juice and pepper on veal. Moisten bread slightly with water. Sauté onions, ham or ground beef, and parsley in 1 tablespoon of shortening for 15 minutes. Add this mixture to the bread. Add eggs, sausage, salt, and pepper. Mix thoroughly. Fill veal pocket with stuffing and secure. Put on rack in shallow pan. Roast for 10 minutes. Reduce oven temperature to 375° and roast for 1½ hours, frequently basting with juices.

GREEKS

The Greeks have been an important part of Florida's history, having been one of the first non-English ethnic groups to settle here. During the two decades of British control of Florida (1763–1783), the British tried various means of organizing settlements and establishing plantations to make the colony profitable. One enterprising Scottish physician, Dr. Andrew Turnbull, wanted to grow indigo in the area below Daytona Beach. To do so, he imported more than fourteen hundred indentured laborers from the Mediterranean area, including Minorcans and four hundred Greeks. He named the Florida settlement New Smyrna Beach after his Greek wife's hometown of Smyrna, Turkey. After eventually abandoning the New Smyrna Beach plantation for St. Augustine, the Greeks settled down and prospered. Today, the city's St. Photios Greek Orthodox National Shrine commemorates the trials of those first Greeks in Florida.

Another thriving Greek enclave in this state was at Tarpon Springs on the west coast of Florida. Greek spongers arrived in the early twentieth century to dive for sponges in the Gulf of Mexico and establish one of the most ethnic towns in Florida, one that is closely associated with Greece to this day.

While these residents, many of whom speak fluent Greek and practice the Greek Orthodox religion, celebrate religious feasts in ways reminiscent of their homeland, they also celebrate Christmas, albeit in their own unique way, often combining Greek and American traditions. In fact, families usually celebrate three holidays at this time of the year: Christmas, New Year's, and the most important one, Epiphany.

In Greek communities such as Tarpon Springs, Greek-American children go through the streets singing carols and spreading good cheer on Christmas Eve and New Year's Eve. Whenever they stop in front of a house to sing carols, the residents usually come out and give the children presents. As in Greece, the red-robed, white-bearded Santa Claus may be replaced by someone looking like St. Basil, who is also honored on New Year's Day.

One of the favorite carols the children sing is "*Ti chara!*" ("Jingle Bells"):

> *Ti chara, ti chara, ti chara paidia*
> *Elthan ta Christougenna me geloia kai chara*
> *Ti chara ti chara elthen o Christos*
> *Kai mazu tou ephthasen o philos Santa Klos.*

Greek families usually visit one another at this time of the year, wishing each other "*Kala Christouyenna*" ("Merry Christmas"), exchanging gifts, eating pastries, and drinking Greek coffee. The most important part of the celebration is the church service, which also includes caroling. Afterwards, the families return home and enjoy some coffee with *tiropitas* (cheese-filled filo triangles) and *spanikopitas* (spinach-filled triangles). On Christmas Eve, the cooks spend much time preparing a special meal for the next day. The family may have been fasting up to that point and will be ready to partake of the turkey or pig that they have been fattening for weeks. One of the special breads is called *christopsomo* (Christ bread), which is made in large, sweet loaves in different shapes and with different images carved on the crusts, images that represent some aspect of the family's life and work.

One of the carols that the Greeks sing on Christmas Eve and Christmas Day is "*The Kalanta*" ("The Carols"), which has the following stanza in English: "In a cave he is born/In a manger of horses/The King of the Heavens/And the Creator of everything." A specially blessed, round bread prepared for the occasion, *christopsomo,* has a cross on top with a walnut inside and four walnuts or almonds at the ends. Often, godmothers prepare small dolls to give to their godchildren. The children from the Sunday School will present a Nativity play.

The main meal on Christmas Day might include stuffed partridge and quail or *kleftiko* (lamb). The meat bakes three or four hours in a clay pot. Desserts include *baklava, kalaktobouriko* (rum cake), and wreath-shaped *koulourakia* (nut rolls). A special treat is *kourabiedes* (holiday butter cookies). The families pay special heed to the poor on that day, making sure to give the first slice of the Christmas loaf to the first beggar passing by the house.

Seven days later, on New Year's Eve, the children walk through the streets, asking people if they want the carolers to sing about St. Basil, who is honored on New Year's Day as the first person to establish an orphanage for little children and the first Christian hospital. The tradition of honoring St. Basil on Christmas Day began about sixteen hundred years ago when he outwitted a bad ruler in Caesarea.

The ruler had demanded that the people pay him twice as much in taxes as they were supposed to. The people then went to Bishop Vassilios (Basil) and asked for his help. The bishop had the people donate treasures, including gold coins, which he then presented to the ruler, who was so moved by the people and Basil that he would not take any of the coins. When Basil wanted to return the treasures to their rightful owners, he did not know who had contributed what, so he had the people make small *pitas* (loaves of bread). Inside the loaves he put the treasures, then gave the loaves to the people. As the people cut open the bread, they all found exactly what they had previously donated to Basil.

In honor of St. Basil, Greek-Americans prepare similar loaves of bread, called *vasilopita* (sweet bread of St. Basil), and put a coin inside each loaf. Those who find a coin in their piece of bread are supposed to have good luck in the coming year. The sweets that are added to the bread symbolize the sweetness and joy of everlasting life, as well as the hope that the coming year will be full of sweetness, health, and happiness for all who participate in the *vasilopita* observance.

When the Greek congregation observes the *vasilopita* at church, the priest cuts out portions of the special bread and dedicates them to Christ, His Holy Church, the patriarch, archbishop, bishop, clergy, and laity. The money collected at the ceremony is sent to the Children's Home of St. Basil's Academy in Garrison, New York.

When they go from house to house singing carols, the children often bring with them little boats or churches they have made out of cardboard. The people drop a coin into the boats or churches, which the children display with much pride. The people at each house might also give refreshments like *melomakarona* (New Year cookies) to the children, who wish everyone "*Chronia polla*" ("Many happy returns") as they accompany their singing with a small drum, a metal triangle, and a mouth organ.

Some Greek-Americans believe that the first person who enters the house on New Year's Day will bring good luck during the year, so they make sure that person is the master of the house or the eldest son or some other important person. Others break a pomegranate in front of the main door, wishing the house to be as full of goods that year as the pomegranate is full of seeds.

The Twelfth Day of Christmas, the Feast of the Epiphany, is commemorated with elaborate ceremonies. This holiday commemorates the baptism of Christ in the River Jordan, when the faithful believe that the Holy Spirit descended on Christ in the form of a dove. The Greek Orthodox community believes that this holiday is more important than others because it reveals the divine nature of Christ. Again, distant relatives and friends may gather at one place for good conversation, games, and a meal. One of the highlights of the meal is again the *vasilopita* with hidden Greek coins.

On The Feast of the Epiphany (January 6) in Tarpon Springs, the archbishop or some other distinguished bishop, assisted by the priest stationed at the Orthodox Church of Nicholas, leads the religious festivities, which include the Blessing of the Waters and prayers for calm seas and the safety of all sailors, as well as blessings for all of the faithful. The clergy and congregation then proceed to Spring Bayou, where they release a white dove symbolizing the Holy Spirit. The archbishop then tosses a golden cross into the bayou, and the young Greek men of the community leap into the water from their boats to frantically search the bottom of the lake for the cross. The one who retrieves it is believed to have a year of good fortune ahead of him.

Afterwards, most people proceed downtown for a *glendi*, an afternoon of Greek food, dancing, and socializing, to be followed in the evening by the formal Epiphany Ball. Thousands of people take part in the ceremony, which is primarily religious and attracts many visitors. This brings an end to the Christmas celebrations for the year, one of the longest periods among ethnic groups in Florida.

VASILOPITA (SWEET BREAD OF ST. BASIL)

2 oz. yeast

1 pt. warm milk, divided
½ tsp. salt
3 lbs. flour, divided
4 oz. melted butter
6 eggs
½ tsp. sesame seeds
3 oz. sugar
¼ cup of almonds
1 tsp. cinnamon

Put the yeast into a mixing bowl. Add half the milk, the salt, and 4 tablespoons of flour. Cover with a cloth and leave in a warm place for an hour to let the batter rise. Put the rest of the flour in another mixing bowl, stir in the yeast batter, and add the butter, 5 eggs, sesame seeds, and the rest of the milk. Mix thoroughly. Knead for 10 minutes. If the dough is too stiff, add more milk; if too mushy, add more flour. Cover the dough again and let it sit for 3 hours. When it has risen, place it on a floured board and knead. Shape it into the form of a loaf. Put this into a greased baking tin with enough room for it to rise. Take part of the dough, roll it into the shape of a long sausage, and place on the top of the loaf. Cover the dough again and let it rise another inch, then put a coin into the dough. Beat the last egg with warm water and sugar; brush this over the top of the dough. Sprinkle chopped almonds and cinnamon over the top. Place dough into the oven. Bake in a moderate oven until brown.

HISPANICS

Hispanics make up one of the largest ethnic groups in Florida, accounting for approximately two million people out of a population of over fifteen million. The term "Hispanic" covers a wide variety of Spanish-speaking people from different countries, all of them having customs that are similar in some respects and different in others.

One of the largest groups of Hispanics are Cuban immigrants, many of whom curtailed their holiday celebrations in Cuba when dictator Fidel Castro banned the celebration of Christmas in 1969 because it supposedly interfered with the sugar harvest. In Florida, those immigrants can once again celebrate the Feast of the Nativity, as they had done for centuries.

The most important dinner of the year for Hispanics is on Christmas Eve, or *Noche Buena* ("Good Night"). If Thanksgiving is a time for roast turkey, *Noche Buena* is a time for *lechon* (roast pork), which marinates for days in a sour-orange and seasoning sauce called *mojo*. The meal also includes black beans, rice, plantains, and, for dessert, *pastelitos* (pastries), *turrones* (nougats), and flan. But different Hispanic groups prepare their meals differently. For example, while many Cubans prepare their pork rotisserie-style or cook it in a *caja china* (Chinese box) over coals, Dominicans (those from the Dominican Republic) prepare an oven roast. Because Catholicism is stronger in the Dominican Republic than in Cuba—no doubt because of Cuba's restrictions on religion—Cubans in Florida have their big Christmas Eve dinner at the stroke of midnight, while Dominicans, determined to focus on the celebration of the birth of Christ, eat their dinner a few hours earlier so they can attend Midnight Mass. Those Florida families with one parent from Cuba and the other from the Dominican Republic will alternate and have midnight dinner one year and Midnight Mass the other.

Cubans love *salsa* music, and Dominicans love the *merengue*. On *Noche Buena*, everyone likes to dance, and, as the night wears on, recorded music is replaced by live music, especially the guitar. Soon everyone is singing, especially after imbibing a glass of rum or *liquor crema*, a creamy drink resembling eggnog.

No matter how late people stay up on Christmas Eve, they all try to rise early on Christmas morning to wish each other "*Feliz Navidad*" ("Merry Christmas") and open presents. Children believe that Santa brings them presents on Christmas Day and the Three Kings bring them presents on January 6. But, while Hispanic children do not usually leave Santa milk and cookies, they do leave "hay" (often grass from the yard) and water for the camels of the Three Kings.

January 6 is commemorated as the day when the Three Kings went to Bethlehem with gifts of gold, frankincense, and myrrh for the Christ child. On that day, called *El Dia de los Reyes Magos*, family members exchange presents with one another. The children may have written letters to the Three Wise Men, asking for specific presents, just as other children write to Santa Claus in the weeks before Christmas. A special Nativity procession with floats of gifts takes place in the evening, followed by midnight church services and festive parties.

Although Three Kings' Day is celebrated throughout Latin America and wherever Hispanics live in Florida, how it is celebrated varies from place to place. Those from Mexico celebrate by breaking a large loaf of crusty bread called *Rosca de Reyes*. The cook hides a small figurine of Baby Jesus in the bread; the person who finds it is supposed to host a party on February 2, the religious holiday when Mary and Joseph, the parents of Jesus, presented him in the temple.

Among the special Mexican foods prepared for the celebration of Three Kings' Day is a special king's cake, consisting of yeast bread and cherries with crystallized fruit and sugar. Another favorite that day is *tamales* (cornmeal patties stuffed with corn), vegetables, and meat. The favorite beverage is *atole*, made of milk, water, sugar, and cornmeal. Then Mexican chocolates end the meal.

CUBAN-STYLE ROAST PORK

1 2-lb. leg of pork
3 garlic cloves, cut into pieces
Salt and paprika for seasoning
Juice of 2 sour oranges or 4 limes

Preheat oven to 525°. Cut slices into the leg of pork and stuff them with the garlic, salt, and paprika. Rub the rest of the cloves and paprika over the outside of the pork and pour the citrus juice over it. Cover the pork with aluminum foil and roast it in the oven for 30 minutes; lower the temperature to 350°, remove the foil, and cook for 30 more minutes. Serves four.

ITALIANS

Florida has managed to attract many Italian immigrants, whether directly from Italy or from other states. Tampa, for example, was a favorite place because of cigar-making factories where immigrants could work.

Christmas for many Italian-Americans is more of a religious holiday than a commercial one, with everyone wishing each other *"Buone Feste Natalizie"* ("Merry Christmas") and waiting until the Epiphany (January 6) to exchange gifts, although in recent decades children have begun expecting gifts on Christmas. Families try to attend Midnight Mass on Christmas and later eat traditional foods like *panettone* (bread with currants and candied fruit), nut brittle, and *torrone* (nougat candy). In recent decades, the Christmas tree has made its way into Italian homes, but typically families erect the crèche (Nativity scene).

Italians in Florida who celebrate Christmas in a traditional way often have a special meal on Christmas Eve, harking back to the early days of Christianity, when Italians fasted or abstained from meat in order to better prepare themselves to commemorate the birth of Christ. Catholics drank only water before they received Holy Communion at Midnight Mass. The meal that ended the fast was called *Cena della Vigilia* (the dinner of the vigil) and included a variety of fishes. *Cena della Vigilia,* at which family and friends would gather, might take several hours to finish and would culminate in attendance at Midnight Mass.

Even if fasting is no longer observed on Christmas Eve, many Italian families still partake in an all-fish dinner, especially one that includes eel, because they believe that eating eel on Christmas Eve will bring happiness during the coming year. Cooks cut the eel into chunks and bake it with olive oil, bay leaves, and salt. Other favorite dishes among Florida Italians are baccala, octopus, stone crabs, clams, mussels, calamari, shrimp, lobster, scallops, capellini with a tuna tomato sauce, and seafood salad. The number of fish served differs according to family custom, whether just three kinds, in honor of the Three Wise Men; seven, in honor of the seven sacraments; or thirteen, for Jesus and His twelve disciples.

Those who follow Christmas customs from Italy may have variations on American customs. For example, to many Italian-Americans, the *presepio* (manger or crib), because it represents in miniature the Holy Family in the stable, becomes the centerpiece of Christmas, with family members and guests kneeling and musicians singing in front of it. The figures in the tiny manger are usually hand-carved and very detailed in features and dress.

Many Italian families have their big meal at midday on Christmas Day, beginning with champagne followed by antipasto, tortellini, chestnuts, fish or turkey, *torrone,* and *panettone.*

PANETTONE

1 package dry active yeast
¼ cup lukewarm milk
8 tbs. of butter
⅓ cup sugar
3 eggs

3 cups all-purpose flour
½ teaspoon salt
4 tbs. of shredded almonds
8 tbs. seedless raisins
6 tbs. diced citron
1 egg yolk
1 tsp. water

Mix the yeast with the lukewarm milk. Set aside until the yeast softens. Cream the butter with the sugar until they are completely blended. Beat the eggs to a froth. Slowly stir the eggs into the butter-sugar blend. Sift the flour with the salt in a large bowl. Add softened yeast. Blend in the butter-sugar-egg mixture. Add more milk if necessary. Cover a pastry board with a light sprinkling of flour. Put dough onto the board and knead until it is smooth. Add more flour if the dough is sticky. Dust a bowl lightly with flour. Place the dough into the bowl. Wrap a slightly moistened towel over the bowl. Allow the dough to rise in a warm place until it doubles in size (about 2 hours). Take the dough out and knead it again for 5 minutes. Place it back into the bowl, cover it, and let it rise again to double its size (about 1 hour).

Roll the dough out flat on the pastry board with a rolling pin. Mix the almonds, raisins, and citron together and spread the mixture on top of the dough. Bring both ends of the dough to the center, press them down, and roll out the dough again until it is flat. Repeat process of folding and flattening the dough. Shape the dough into a ball with your hands. Place the ball into a deep, buttered pan that is twice as large as the ball of dough. Cover the dough and let it double in size again (about 1 hour). Preheat oven to 350°. Beat the egg yolk with water. Brush this mixture over the dough. Bake in preheated oven for 30–40 minutes. When the *pannetone* turns golden brown, remove it from the oven and loosen it with a thin, sharp knife.

MINORCANS

When the British controlled Florida in the eighteenth century (1763–1783), they tried to populate the peninsula with settlers, especially those willing to farm the land. One ill-conceived plan was to transplant hundreds of Mediterranean people, under the leadership of Scottish physician Dr. Andrew Turnbull, to what became known as New Smyrna Beach. Many from the island of Minorca became indentured laborers, who made the trip to Florida with high expectations and hopes but were soon disappointed.

The Minorcans had many conflicts with the harsh Dr. Turnbull. Because he was from Great Britain and they were from the Mediterranean, different customs caused problems. For example, because the British considered Christmas the most important holiday of the year, they gave their workers three days off at Christmas and encouraged what has been termed "much frolic." But the Minorcans had far more important religious holidays (they considered Christmas to be no more important than any other saint's day). While they no doubt appreciated the time off from the harsh conditions under which they worked, they probably would have been happier to exchange the Christmas respite for one at another time.

After the Minorcans abandoned New Smyrna Beach and settled in St. Augustine in 1777, they became an integral part of that city and remain so today. One unusual custom they practiced in St. Augustine around Christmastime, especially from 1784 to1786, was to restrict weddings to December in order to make it easy for newly arrived priests to perform the weddings at one time. One result of such a custom was a number of loud parties around Christmastime that saw people dressing in grotesque masquerades and making a lot of noise, protected by the anonymity of their disguises.

Several works describe the Minorcans, including Jane Quinn's *Minorcans in Florida* (1975) and Patricia C. Griffin's *Mullet on the Beach* (1991). In "Christmas in Old St. Augustine" (*Florida Living*, December 1984) Eileen Ronan describes how the Minorcans celebrate Christmas with special foods, including a fruitcake made with four pounds of batter (butter, sugar, flour, and eggs) and eight pounds of fruit, much of which they pick from their own trees.

The Minorcans have a Yule log, cedar boughs, and a Christmas tree trimmed with real candles and popcorn strings. During the holiday season, people visit with neighbors who bring out their fruitcake, to be served with wine or strong coffee. Another favorite food is ground-nut candy or peanuts made from recipes handed down faithfully from mother to daughter. Finally, they make Minorcan bread pudding with a whiskey sauce.

MINORCAN BREAD PUDDING
2½ cups of sugar, divided
6 whole eggs
2 qts. fresh milk
1 tsp. of vanilla, lemon, or walnut extract
5 slices of bread, torn into pieces
1 cup of light raisins
1 apple, peeled and cored
Nutmeg
2 tsp. of cornstarch
½ cup of butter
6 oz. of whiskey (optional)

Set oven to 375°. Mix 1½ cups of sugar, eggs, and milk. Add extract, bread, and raisins. Dice half an apple into the pudding and put the other half on top. Sprinkle nutmeg on top of the pudding and bake it in the oven until it turns golden brown and puffs up.

For the sauce, boil 2½ cups of water. Mix in cornstarch dissolved in cold water, butter, and remaining 1 cup of sugar. Cook over low flame until mixture bubbles and thickens. Stir sauce until it is smooth, then pour it into a large bowl to cool for half an hour. Add whiskey if desired. Pour warm sauce over warm pudding. Serves 4–6 people.

NORWEGIANS

Scandinavians in general and Norwegians in particular have long been associated with Florida. In the nineteenth century, one of the newspapers in the Florida Panhandle, the *Pensacola Commercial*, noted how the local Scandinavians, who had moved there because of the great lumber boom, had their own church and celebrated Christmas in their own European way.

The same newspaper (December 31, 1888) described how the

Scandinavians in the city had celebrated *Yule Festen* the previous night in their church on Palafox Wharf. The church displayed the flags of Norway, Sweden, and Denmark as the sailors of those nations partook of the hospitality of the Pensacolians, who gave them presents and culinary delicacies.

Originally founded in 1895 in Minnesota, the Sons of Norway was organized as a fraternal organization to protect Norwegian-Americans from the financial hardships experienced during times of sickness or death in the family. Over time, the organization has preserved the best of Norwegian heritage and culture in America and today has some 420 local lodges and a membership of sixty-seven thousand people in both North America and Norway. The fifteen Florida lodges of the Sons of Norway are Everglades (Cape Coral), Gateway to Florida (Jacksonville), Gulfstream (Port St. Lucie), Lauderdale (Ft. Lauderdale), Miami (Miami), Norsemen Harbour (Port Charlotte), Palm Coast (Lantana), Port Orange (Port Orange), Sarasota (Sarasota), Scandia (Naples), Space Coast (Indialantic), Sun Viking (Spring Hill), Suncoast (Clearwater), Tampa Bay (Tampa), and Vikingworld (Orlando).

These groups, which meet periodically throughout the year, at Christmastime follow Scandinavian customs—even noting the winter solstice—and often combine them with American traditions. One of the main points of a Norwegian Christmas, whether celebrated in Scandinavia or Florida, is that Norwegians open their gifts on Christmas Eve instead of Christmas morning.

At the local lodge of the Sons of Norway, the annual Christmas party for the children starts with adults and children circling the Christmas tree, holding hands, singing American and Norwegian carols, and wishing each other *"God Jul"* or *"Gledelig Jul."* Later, the *Julenisse* (Santa Claus) arrives to join in the festivities and distribute gifts to the children. Some lodges have a celebration for children in the afternoon and other festivities for the adults in the evening.

The Christmas tree is an important part of holiday celebrations for Norwegian-Americans, probably more so than for Norwegians in the old country since the Christmas tree was not introduced into Norway from Germany until the second half of the nineteenth century. Also, in Norway the parents usually decorated the tree on Christmas Eve behind the closed doors of the living room, while the children waited with much anticipation outside the room.

Today in this country, the *Juletree* (Christmas tree), whether at the lodge or at home, is usually put in the center of a large room and decorated with gold and silver balls and food. The participants form rings around the tree, with the smallest children in the inner ring and the adults in the outer ring. Everyone then walks around the tree singing carols; at a given signal, everyone stops and takes one item off the tree, a practice that continues until all that remains are paper items and the gold and silver balls. Some of the trees have *julekurv*, woven, heart-shaped baskets that hold hard candies and raisins.

Another item on the tree is *det rene flagg* (Norwegian flag), a reminder to Norwegian-Americans of the long struggle that Norway had in disengaging itself from Danish rule and Swedish union. Such flags became especially important when the occupying Nazi forces during World War II forbade displays of the Norwegian flag.

Another of the Norwegian symbols still used in some Florida homes are the straw decorations representing the Old World practice of using straw to ward off the *oskerei* (evil spirits) that roamed the earth looking for the *juleøl* (Christmas beer), which was stored hidden from view in the *stabbur*. A farm's inhabitants would sleep on the straw-covered floor of the main house on Christmas Eve, a favorite time for the *oskerei* to wander the earth and also a time when everyone would remember the straw-filled manger where Christ was born.

As with many ethnic groups in Florida, food plays a major part of holiday festivities. The main course for Christmas Eve dinner may include fresh ham (baked with the thick skin of the pig scored into diamond shapes), creamed cabbage, boiled potatoes, lingonberry jam, and gravy. For dessert, there is *Julekake* (a type of stollen), several different kinds of Christmas cookies, and coffee.

Some families have a *julebord* (Christmas buffet), especially for large groups of people. The table features *surkål* (sweet-and-sour cabbage), several kinds of meat and seafood with sauces, *lefse* (thin potato flat bread), salads, and vegetables. Desserts include puddings, creams, mousse, cookies, and *kransekake* (wreath cake). Other foods Norwegian-Americans prepare at Christmastime include various pork or ham dishes, seven kinds of cookies, and *risengrynsgrøt* (rice porridge). The adults may wash it down with *juleøl*. Those who have the time will prepare dishes from scratch, but these Norwegian specialties are also available from bakeries and grocery stores. As is true in Norway, foods prepared at Florida lodges differ from place to place.

RISENGRYNSGRØT (RICE PORRIDGE)
⅔ cup uncooked rice
1⅔ cups water
4 cups of boiling milk
1½ tsp. of butter
Salt
Milk, cinnamon, and sugar to taste

Slowly pour rice into boiling water and stir until mixture returns to a boil. Cover container. Cook slowly until most of the water is absorbed by the rice. Stir in boiling milk. Simmer until the rice is tender and the porridge has thickened, which takes about 1½ hours. Add butter and salt. Serve hot with milk, cinnamon, and sugar on top.

SCOTS

Several Florida cities, such as Dunedin, Ocala, Orlando, Tallahassee, Tampa, and West Palm Beach, have Scottish-American or St. Andrew's Societies, groups of people interested in knowing more about and preserving their Scottish heritage. Named after the first disciple of Christ to identify Him as the Messiah, the societies often sponsor Highland Games and Scottish festivals throughout the year.

While Florida Scots celebrate Christmas Eve and Christmas Day the traditional American way [though they wish each other *"Nollaig chridheil huibh"* ("Merry Christmas" in Scots Gaelic)], they do have a special holiday, Hogmanay, that they celebrate on New Year's Eve. At a typical Hogmanay Party, families bring a covered dish either to someone's home or to a rented facility. All wear their Scottish finery: the men in their kilts and the women in long dresses or long kilted skirts. There is Scottish country dancing and an old-fashioned *ceilidh* (party), during which everyone gets up and does a party piece: tells a joke, poem, or story; dances; sings a song; or plays an instrument. At the stroke of midnight, everyone joins in a circle and sings "Auld Lang Syne" by the great Scottish poet Robert Burns.

One dish associated with this time of year is the delicious Dundee Cake.

DUNDEE CAKE

½ lb. softened butter, divided
2½ cups all-purpose flour, divided
1 cup sugar
5 eggs
¾ cup seedless raisins
¾ cup dried currants
¾ cup mixed candied fruit peel, coarsely chopped
½ cup ground almonds
8 candied cherries, halved
2 tbs. finely grated orange peel
Pinch of salt
1 tsp. baking soda dissolved in 1 tsp. milk
⅓ cup blanched almonds, split lengthwise into halves

Preheat oven to 300°. With a pastry brush, coat the sides and bottom of an 8-by-3-inch springform cake pan with 1 tablespoon of softened butter. Sprinkle 2 tablespoons of flour into the pan and shake pan to coat evenly. Turn the pan over and tap on it to remove any excess flour. In a large mixing bowl, combine remaining butter with sugar until light and fluffy. Beat in the eggs with the flour. Add the raisins, currants, candied peel, ground almonds, cherries, orange peel, and salt. Mix thoroughly. Stir in dissolved baking soda, pour batter into pan, place blanched almonds on top, and bake in middle of oven for 1½ hours. Let cake cool in pan for 5 minutes before cutting. Makes one 8-inch round cake.

CHRISTMAS AROUND THE STATE

BOCA RATON

Each December, about one hundred thousand people turn out along the Intracoastal Waterway in Boca Raton for a boat parade sponsored by the Greater Boca Raton Chamber of Commerce. Several dozen beautifully decorated boats, ranging in length from a few feet to a few hundred feet, participate in the annual holiday tradition. Silver Palm Park and Red Reef Park have bleachers for spectators, while other places along the waterway also accommodate the thousands of visitors for the free event. The parade creates a festive atmosphere for the holiday season and demonstrates that Santa can arrive by boat rather than by sleigh.

Other Florida sites with boat parades are Cape Coral, Cocoa Beach, DeLand, Dunedin, Fanning Springs, Ft. Lauderdale, Jacksonville, Key Largo, Kissimmee, Madeira Beach, Miami, North Miami Beach, Palm Coast, Pensacola, Pompano Beach, Punta Gorda, Riverview, St. Augustine, St. Petersburg, Titusville, Venice, Vero Beach, West Palm Beach, and Winter Haven.

Santa might arrive by boat or plane.
Florida State Archives

BROOKSVILLE

Rogers' Christmas House and Village is one of several places throughout the state that specialize in holiday-related goods. Part business, part tourist attraction, the site attracts some four hundred thousand people throughout the year. The busiest times are the two weekends after Thanksgiving. The Christmas House Village includes five large houses, each decorated in a special way. The Storybook Land House, for example, has themes from storybooks, Santa's Workshop, and even a Halloween Room.

The store originated in the early 1950s as Ghiotto's Gift Shop attached to Rogers' Department Store, making it the original Christmas House. It moved to the Rogers' home briefly after the store was sold, then reopened in 1972 at its present location. Visitors can find tree ornaments, elaborate stockings, blown glass, candelabra—almost all with a Christmas theme. Those who prefer not to shop or who need to recuperate from shopping can rest in the dozen rocking chairs in front of the main building. Youngsters in particular can enjoy Storybook Land in the nearby flowered courtyard, where life-sized characters from Cinderella, Jack and the Beanstalk, Sleeping Beauty, and The Wizard of Oz are on display.

Open 9:30 a.m. to 5 p.m. every day of the year except Christmas. Phone: (352) 796-2415. Address: 103 South Saxon Avenue. Brooksville

Santa's elves work near banana plants at Rogers' Christmas House in Brooksville.
Kevin McCarthy

is about ten miles west of busy I-75, which has large billboards advertising the Christmas House. Web site: www.rogerschristmashouse.com

Seminole Studios at 460 Hancock Lake Road in Brooksville is a good example of a card company that has taken advantage of its location to produce Christmas cards with a Florida theme. Named after its original location (Seminole, Florida) and its print shop (Seminole Press), the company was looking for ways to increase its business during the slow summer months. The owners, the Roses, found a struggling Christmas card company in Miami and were all set to buy it, but the owner told them that he wanted to sell to Miami residents.

At that point, the Roses decided to develop a Christmas card company of their own: they enlisted a Clearwater artist, hired a salesman, and developed a Florida motif for the cards. For the past twenty-five years, the company has been producing the cards, which are very popular among residents and visitors alike. For further information, call (352) 796-7406 or fax (352) 796-1708.

CHRISTMAS

The unincorporated town of Christmas on State Road 50 takes its name from the nearby fort. In fact, the town was called Fort Christmas until the Post Office Department dropped the "Fort" around 1892, when the Christmas Post Office was established. In the early days, the son of the postmaster carried the mail on his back twice a week from the town of Chuluota, twelve miles north, after it had arrived from Sanford by train. Juanita Tucker, who became postmaster in 1932, began the custom of using a special Christmas seal on mail sent from the central Florida town. At first, a cachet with green holly leaves and two bells was used. In 1934, she introduced the famous "Little Green Christmas Tree" rubber-stamp cachet. Two years later, the words "Christmas Greetings" and the year were added below the tree. The wording changed slightly in the following years:

> "Merry Christmas/1937"
> "Yuletide Greetings/1938"
> "A Joyous Christmas/1939"
> "Christmas Cheer/1940"
> "Greetings from Christmas/1941"

After World War II, the wording changed again:

"Peace on Earth/1945"
"Good Will toward Men/1946"
"For the Healing/of the Nations/One World Indivisible/1947"

Postmistress J.S. Tucker, shown here in 1946, was busy in December.
Florida State Archives

In 1948 and 1949, a line from the first Christmas carol, "Glory to God/In the Highest," was used. In 1950, "Glory to God/In the Highest" was moved to a place above the tree, and "Christmas, Orange Co., Fla./1950" appeared below. That basic format, with slight variations, was used through 1980.

In 1981, the little green tree cachet remained, but the year was dropped for good. In 1990, a larger Christmas tree was introduced without a greeting, and only the words "Christmas, Florida" appeared below the tree.

Today, the post office, located at 23580 East Colonial Drive (State Highway 50), can expect over 250,000 pieces of mail to be sent there before being stamped with the little green Christmas tree and sent on their way. Those who want to have their cards stamped

Mailing Christmas cards in Christmas, Florida
Kevin McCarthy

with the "Christmas, Florida" postmark can bring them to the post office or send them already stamped and addressed to: Postmaster, Christmas, FL 32709-9998. Because of the huge volume of cards and letters, the Postmaster can apply the Christmas Tree cachet only to holiday mail received in Christmas before December 10 (although all mail is post-marked "Christmas, FL"). Customers can also apply the "Little Green

Christmas Tree" cachet, which is available on business days during regular business hours, to their envelopes themselves.

To ensure that the postmark is clearly noticeable to those receiving the cards and letters, senders should put only the stamp and address on the front of the envelope, and place the return address on the back flap. The Postal Service recommends that pre-addressed, stamped cards be sent via Priority Mail or Express Mail. Customers may drop off or send cards early with a request to hold for a postmark at a specified later date, provided it is a regular business day for the post office. For any questions, call the Christmas Post Office at (407) 568-2941.

A Peace Garden across the highway from the Christmas Post Office, where State Roads 50 and 420 meet, has a large Christmas tree and permanent manger scene. The garden, dedicated to the Prince of Peace and to all those who have given their lives for the cause of peace and freedom, offers a quiet place of reflection for the many motorists driving along the highway. The stones in the door of the manger come from all fifty states, and the stones in the shrine behind the Nativity come from other countries and historic sites.

The permanent Christmas tree in the Peace Garden has actually been several trees. First decorated in 1952 as it stood next to the post office on Highway 50, it could not survive the hot lights of the decorations and soon perished. A replacement was found, along with two spares, and the townspeople once again decorated it. The tree grew to a height of twenty-five feet, but in 1959, a road crew carelessly damaged it when they let a large pine tree fall on it. However, workers soon had the damaged tree wired up and redecorated to hide the scars.

The next year, Hurricane Donna came through and stripped off all the ornaments from the tree, but it stood tall and survived the storm. The community continued the tradition of lighting the tree and singing carols on the first Sunday in December.

In 1969, when the tree was scheduled to be used on the official First-Day Cover and Program, workers discovered that the tree was dying from the wires that had been placed in and around it years before. The workers quickly cut down the tree, decorated a spare one, and covered up the damaged turf in time for the big celebration.

The following year, when Highway 50 was widened to accommodate increasing traffic, the tree had to be moved from where it stood in the middle of the new right-of-way. Workers replanted it in a safer place, but it did not survive the move, so a new tree was planted in its place. One of the most photographed trees in the country, it continues to inspire many who pass by on the busy highway.

COCOA

Like many planetariums throughout the state at Christmastime, the Astronaut Memorial Planetarium and Observatory at Brevard Community College in Cocoa has a seasonal presentation in December. Entitled "The Alien Who Stole Christmas," it features the adventures of a certain jolly old elf who embarks upon a tour of the solar system with a green-skinned, yellow-eyed pilot of an Unidentified Flying Object (UFO). Contact the planetarium at 1519 Clearlake Road for more information. Phone: (407) 634-3732.

The Brevard Museum of History and Natural Science in Cocoa often has exhibits about early Christmases in the area, including many early toys. Phone: (321) 632-1830.

DAYTONA BEACH

Another timely planetarium show presented in December is at the Museum of Arts and Sciences at 1040 Museum Boulevard, west of downtown Daytona. Produced by Loch Ness Productions and called "'Tis the Season," it traces the development of many of the world's well-known holiday customs, especially those involving lights: the burning Yule log, the lighted Christmas tree, the menorah, and luminarias. The show describes the historical, religious, and cultural rituals practiced during the winter solstice—including Celtic, pagan, Nordic, Roman, Egyptian, Hopi, Jewish, and Christian rites—and explores the possible astronomical explanations for a star over Bethlehem at the time of Christ's birth. For further information about times and fees, call (904) 255-0285.

FORT CHRISTMAS

About thirty-five miles east of Orlando and its crowded theme parks is Fort Christmas, a reconstructed fort from the Seminole Wars, during which federal troops fought Native Americans in what was then the Territory of Florida. In the decade after the United States acquired Florida from Spain in 1821, white settlers from the North moved into the vast farm and pasture lands of the peninsula, an act that soon brought them into conflict with the Native Americans who were already there. From 1817 until 1858, the U.S. government waged three wars with Native Americans. In the longest of those conflicts, the Second Seminole War (1835–1842), federal troops built many forts in central Florida to house soldiers and settlers who needed protection during Indian raids.

Soldiers began construction of the fort on Christmas Day 1837 (hence its name), and it served as a supply depot for the troops waging war against the Indians. As the Indians retreated to the south, the fort lost its importance and was abandoned.

In the 1970s, Jay Blanchard, military historian and director of the Orange County Parks Department, began plans to reconstruct the military installation as a bicentennial project. Today visitors can examine the block houses of the fort and see exhibits and artifacts from the Second Seminole War time period. The reconstructed fort is approximately two miles from where the original one stood, but that site is on private property and not open to the public.

The park also has restored pioneer homes, a Cracker homestead cabin, outhouses, a sugar cane mill, syrup kettle, and other artifacts from the late nineteenth century through the early twentieth century. Annual festivities include two militia encampments, in which soldiers in 1840s-period costume set up camp and present programs in the fort, including musket- and cannon-firing demonstrations; a tree trimming party; a Cracker Christmas celebration, including pioneer demonstrations, a large crafts fair, and exhibits; and a Coronado wireless event, in which ham radio operators set up their equipment and send holiday greetings to all parts of the world. Other events include a cowboy reunion, Fort Christmas Bluegrass Festival, Old Timer's Day, Pioneer Homecoming, and history camp.

The fort and museum, at 1300 Fort Christmas Road (State Road 420), two miles north of State Road 50, are open Tuesday–Saturday, 10 a.m.–5 p.m.; Sunday, 1 p.m.–5 p.m. Admission is free. Pioneer tours are offered Tuesday–Saturday, 11–3, and Sunday, 1–3. Phone: (407) 568-4149.

FT. LAUDERDALE

Winterfest, a special Christmas event in south Florida, particularly Ft. Lauderdale, is a holiday festival featuring a variety of family-centered events, most of which take place in December. A lighted Boat Parade and shoreline decorating along the Intracoastal Waterway, a black-tie ball, and the Grand Marshal Reception make up the major Winterfest components. The parade, usually held in early December, has almost one hundred entries and includes entertainment, stars, and music. It usually follows a route from Port Everglades in Ft. Lauderdale to Lake Santa Barbara in Pompano.

FT. MYERS

The Edison-Ford Winter Estates in Ft. Myers take on a very festive appearance each Christmas. The Ft. Myers Woman's Community Club transforms the estates of Thomas Edison and Henry Ford into a gala show of tasteful decorations known as the Holiday House. The theme changes from year to year, but the more than forty thousand visitors are always amazed at the display of one million lights, the enchanted winter wonderland with Old Man Winter, and even some snow. The Holiday Store sells handmade gifts, including ornaments, tree skirts, and special-recipe preserves. Proceeds go to the Edison & Ford Winter Estates Foundation for restoration and preservation of the buildings.

The days of the event vary each year, but the houses are open most of December except Christmas Eve and Christmas Day. Local school, civic, and religious groups provide complimentary entertainment nightly under the banyan tree. Hours: 5 p.m.–9 p.m. Admission fee. Phone: (941) 334-3614.

JACKSONVILLE

Like other cities throughout Florida and the nation, Jacksonville takes care at Christmastime to provide hot meals and shelter to those less fortunate. For example, the City Rescue Mission, the Clara White Mission, and the Salvation Army, helped by hundreds of volunteers and many goods from religious and community organizations, serve meals to the needy and help provide shelter, especially on the particularly cold nights that Florida sometimes has in December.

For thousands of local children who might not have many Christmas presents, several organizations provide annual parties. For example, at the annual Dorcas Drake Christmas Party, which has been held for over forty years, parents and children start lining up at places like Club Five in Five Points in the wee hours of the morning. As many as four thousand children and parents have been helped because of the generosity of local citizens and businesses.

A snowman contest with imported snow.
Tampa-Hillsborough County Public Library System

Contributions from City Hall and corporate sponsors have made possible cheery Christmases for thousands of children, many of whom are bused in from apartment complexes to the Prime Osborn Convention Center. Even when the gifts for the overflow crowd begin to run out, organizations like the U.S. Marines' Toys for Tots program come through so that none of the children leave without a present.

KEY LARGO

This town and others like it in the Florida Keys sometimes have reenactments of early Christmases. The Historical Preservation Society of the Upper Keys has sponsored a depiction of what the holiday used to be like in the 1800s and early 1900s. As part of their Olde Timers' Christmas, the participants, like the early settlers in the Keys, decorated a Spanish stopper tree with red and white berries found in the neighboring woods, as well as seashells and ornaments washed up on the beaches from shipwrecks or thrown overboard from passing ships. Visitors can also sample old Conch recipes. For more information, contact the Historical Society at P.O. Box 2200, Key Largo, FL 33037.

KEY WEST

The Ernest Hemingway Home and Museum, at 907 Whitehead Street is open during the Christmas holidays but has only minimal holiday decorations. Visitors usually go to the home to see the place where author Ernest Hemingway lived from 1928 through 1940 and wrote several of his novels and stories. Open daily, 9 a.m.–5 p.m. Phone: (305) 294-1136. Web site: www.hemingwayhome.com.

LAKELAND

While many families honor departed loved ones in small, ordinary ways, an extended Lakeland family displays thousands of Christmas lights each December that serve as a tribute to a relative who died in a 1985 traffic accident.

Among the displays are a horse-drawn wagon with Santa and carolers; a Snoopy-driven surrey; giant trees and stars; bears chasing an elf up a tree; manger scenes; carousels; Santa flying a helicopter; a large angel over a manger scene; horses pulling a stagecoach; flamingos and an alligator pulling sleighs; deer flying through the air; toy soldiers; candy canes; and Santa's toy shop with elves making and decorating a sleigh full of toys. The family also makes a giant snowman out of six rolls of hay, which later becomes food for local horses and cows when the season is over. Visiting children are likely to receive candy from a costumed Santa and Mrs. Claus.

The lights have had unintended results. One woman told the family, "You don't know me, but I want you to know that we weren't going to have any Christmas at all until we saw your lights." Another stranger handed a Christmas card to the family. He told them that he had lost his job before Christmas, then lost his family through divorce. He had placed a gun on the seat next to him and begun driving aimlessly through the rural area, looking for a place to kill himself. When he saw the large display of lights on Chase Road and nearby Ritter Road, he changed his mind, resolved to better himself, and went on to obtain a new job and eventually reconcile with his family.

To reach the display, which is usually lit after December 1, drive north of Lakeland on US 98. Take a left at the Duff Road traffic light. Take a left on Green Road, then a left onto Chase Road till you reach the 7900 block, where you will see the many lights on five acres of adjoining property. The lights stay on till about 9 p.m. on weeknights, later on weekends and Christmas Eve.

LAKE WALES

Three miles north of Lake Wales, on the Florida peninsula's highest point, is Bok Tower Gardens, a national historic landmark visited by thousands of people each year. The bell tower houses one of the world's great carillons, a combination of fifty-seven bronze bells ranging in weight from seventeen pounds to nearly twelve tons. Visitors can hear recitals every day at 3 p.m., as well as clock music every half hour beginning at 10 a.m.

Some years it might even be cold enough for a fire.
Kevin McCarthy

The surrounding, 157-acre garden has thousands of azaleas, camellias, magnolias, and other kinds of flowering plants.

Edward Bok, publisher of *Ladies Home Journal* for many years and Pulitzer Prize–winning author of his autobiography, dedicated the 205-foot-high tower and beautiful gardens to the American people in 1929. Open every day, 8 a.m.–6 p.m. Admission fee. For a schedule of Christmas recital times, call (863) 676-1408. Web page: www.boktower.org.

Near Bok Tower and reached through the gardens is the historic Pinewood Estate, a twenty-room Mediterranean Revival–style villa lavishly decorated for the Christmas holidays. Although normally closed on December 24 and 25, the villa has guided tours on other days that give glimpses of the glamorous lifestyle of the 1930s. Built by C. Austin Buck, vice president of Bethlehem Steel, the 1931 mansion draws more than eight thousand visitors over the Christmas holidays who want to see the elegant decorations of a well-to-do 1930s family. Hours: 10 a.m.–5 p.m. Admission fee. Phone: (863) 676-1408.

LUTZ

Small towns like Lutz, north of Tampa, have often carved themselves a niche in Christmas festivities by offering original plays or exhibits. Members of a group called Citizens for the Old Lutz School put on various exhibits, such as a miniature village with "snow," working lampposts, a lighted church, and a village train. Residents donate a tree ornament for a community tree in the school, and fundraisers sell ornaments that depict Lutz past and present. As in many Florida communities, residents donate toys and nonperishable food items for less fortunate families.

MELBOURNE

Officials at the Kennedy Space Center (KSC) near Melbourne have made the Shuttle Landing Facility (SLF) available for emergency landings by Santa Claus since the SLF opened in the 1970s. The fifteen-thousand-foot-long, three-hundred-foot-wide landing strip is among the world's largest and could provide a welcome haven for Santa Claus in the event of reindeer problems or mechanical difficulties with his new, high-tech sleighs.

Officials at the Space Center believe that Santa has gone to state-of-the-art sleighs in recent years due to the increasing numbers of children and the greater workload this has imposed. His reindeer aren't getting any younger, either, and the new, lighter sleighs are made of composite materials to lighten their burden.

Other recent improvements include better brakes and a braking parachute. Apparently, Santa has also incorporated stealth technology into the new designs to reduce their radar profiles. He is quoted as saying, "I have to make deliveries in countries that are not at peace with one another. Even though the children have behaved themselves, some of the grown-ups' anti-aircraft guns still pose a threat to my reusable launch vehicle."

Officials are quick to point out that the accommodation to Santa's possible landing at the KSC involves no government expense since no personnel will be on duty on Christmas Eve. The automated landing systems will be left on in the automatic mode.

When asked if Santa ever had to make a forced landing at KSC, the SLF manager, who spoke on condition of anonymity, replied: "We have no actual proof, but the morning after a real cold Christmas several years ago we found a twisted sleigh runner we've never been able to account for."

Those interested in tracking Santa on Christmas Eve can log onto the KSC web site (www.ksc.nasa.gov/ksc.html) or the Santa Tracking page (lift.off.msfc.nasa.gov/home/seasonal/SantaTrackHome.html).

MIAMI

As is true in other Florida cities, Miami residents have been most generous in helping the less fortunate each December. *The Miami Herald* publishes true stories about the plight of local residents and has *Herald's* Wish Book, which describes the situations of particular families and solicits funds or in-kind donations for those families. The more than $200,000 that the newspaper raises and the "adoption" of families by local stores and businesses result in the purchase of appliances, clothing, computers, and services for many in need. For example, a malnourished senior citizen might receive a new microwave to help him prepare at least one hot meal a day. Children at local schools often "adopt" another youngster in the community and give that child with presents and goods at Christmastime. Often, a local businessperson matches any funds raised by the children.

Miami-Dade's Infill Housing Initiative and other such programs provide affordable homes to low- and moderate-income families, especially around Christmastime. Officials use county-owned vacant lots in urban neighborhoods and arrange with banks and mortgage companies to provide low-interest loans to those who are chosen for the program.

Because of the many Hispanics in the area, local slaughterhouses are particularly busy in the week before Christmas when those wishing to have a *Noche buena* feast on Christmas Eve handpick the pigs to be prepared for the traditional meal.

Miami International Airport is very busy at Christmastime. The normal 75,000–100,000 daily passengers increases to 95,000–110,000 each of the two days before Christmas as people use the major airport to reach home and their relatives. Employees there make a special effort to ease the congestion of the many flyers.

ORLANDO

For over twenty years the *Sentinel* Santa Program, sponsored by The Orlando Sentinel, has raised money for both needy children and for critical community-based programs throughout the year. Helped by such organizations as the Robert R. McCormick Tribune Foundation, the program consistently raises more money than it did in the previous year, reaching over a million dollars in 1999 alone.

Local residents will often go out to Celebration, the Disney-owned community, to see soap-based snowflakes wafting about in the December air. Others go to local theme parks to see parades and lighted trees. City churches and synagogues, as well as organizations like the Salvation Army and the Orlando Union Rescue Mission, serve meals to hundreds of homeless and less fortunate over the holidays. Members of the Congregation of Liberal Judaism in Orlando often volunteer on Christmas Eve and Christmas Day itself to allow workers at various businesses to be home with their families.

PENSACOLA

Historic Pensacola Village and the T.T. Wentworth Museum decorate their buildings inside and out with festive holiday attire. Their historic homes are available for tours, and they feature children's programming in the Julee Cottage on Saturday mornings from 10 a.m.–1 p.m. Phone: (850) 595-5985.

Escambia County Transit Authority historic trolleys feature narrated evening tours of the downtown area in the weeks prior to Christmas. These tours offer a good overview of Pensacola history as well as a glimpse of the area's Christmas brilliance. Phone: (850) 595-3228.

For music lovers, Pensacola Heritage Foundation sponsors an Evening in Old Seville Square - Christmas Edition prior to Christmas in the gazebo located in the center of historic Seville Square on the shores of Pensacola Bay. The evening features many performers from different genres. Phone: (850) 438-6505.

The Christmas season in Pensacola would not be complete without the much-anticipated annual production of "Christmas on the Coast." Each year, more than two hundred members of the Pensacola Children's Chorus take the stage at the Saenger Theatre and delight audiences with sparkling holiday music, lively movement, and colorful costumes. In the summer of 1995, the Pensacola Children's Chorus was approached to revitalize an annual fundraiser for two local media charities, and the entire gala evening was televised by the local ABC affiliate. "Christmas on the Coast" is now a major component of the Pensacola Children's Chorus season and has become a sold-out, two-night holiday tradition in northwest Florida. The production features well-known carols and seasonal songs, as well as original arrangements by Allen Pote, who with his wife, Susan, is the founding director of the Pensacola Children's Chorus. Over the past ten years, they have seen the chorus grow to its current membership of over two hundred children in four choirs, and they have conducted them in concerts as well as prepared them for performances with other arts organizations in Pensacola, such as the Pensacola Symphony, Pensacola Opera, and Pensacola Choral Society.

Big Lagoon State Recreation Area, to the west of Pensacola and on the mainland across from Perdido Key, has an annual "Christmas in the Park" celebration at the beginning of December. The two-night event attracts thousands of visitors. Activities include storytelling, hayrides, live entertainment, holiday foods, children's activities, and even a visit from Santa himself. For more information, call (850) 492-2785 (Friends of Big Lagoon) or (850) 492-1595 (Big Lagoon Park).

Pensacola Children's chorus presents "Christmas on the Coast"
Pensacola Children's Chorus

PUNTA GORDA

The Punta Gorda Business and Community Alliance some years ago established Holly Days, a festival that includes a tour of selected homes, a garden show, downtown decorations, caroling, a tree-lighting ceremony near the town clock, a play put on by the local high school, a lighted-boat parade near Fishermen's Village, a land-based parade, numerous musical concerts, and many church services.

ST. AUGUSTINE

Beginning in late November and continuing through part of January, St. Augustine has an annual Nights of Lights that attracts thousands of residents and tourists. The city adorns many of its downtown windows, roofs, spires, and trees—even the historic Bridge of Lions and the city's sea walls—with white lights. Also featured are holiday music festivals, arts and crafts, historical reenactments (such as the British Night Watch Ceremony), candlelight Christmas caroling, a parade, sightseeing tours, a Christmas open house at the Castillo de San Marcos, and a Regatta of Lights. For more information, call (800) OLD-CITY (653-2489).

The Lightner Museum, across from Flagler College, usually has displays of old-time Christmases, such as those celebrated in the nineteenth century.

A St. Augstine Christmas parade in 1951.
Florida State Archives

SANFORD

The Seminole Community College Planetarium produces a live show each December called "The Star of Bethlehem," which first looks at the clues from the Bible to help determine the possible birth year(s) of Jesus, then examines what was going on in the sky during those times. The show takes a close look at the Magi, their likely origins, and how they would have viewed signs in the heavens from an astrological rather than an astronomical viewpoint. A commentator discusses what the word "star" meant back then, e.g., "falling star" (meteor), "hairy star" (comet), "new star" (nova), and "appearing star" (conjunction). The show discounts meteors, comets, and novae, then focuses on conjunctions, explaining and demonstrating what they are by using the virtual reality nature of the planetarium. The show demonstrates different theories about the star—specifically whether it was a natural phenomenon or of divine origin—inviting individuals to decide for themselves.

The "Star of Bethlehem" show usually runs every Friday evening between Thanksgiving and Christmas. Also, due to requests from patrons wishing to bring visiting relatives in the summer, special "Christmas in July" showings are offered on the first and fourth Fridays in July. For more information, call (407) 328-2360 to hear a recorded schedule of current shows or (407) 328-2409 to speak with a member of the staff.

Floridians in citrus country enjoyed sending appropriate Christmas cards to their friends in the North.
Florida State Archives.

STUART

The town of Stuart in Martin County has an evening parade on the first Friday of December each year. The floats, based on a different theme each year, are judged for lights, music, and their adherence to the theme. Each year Soroptimist International of Stuart organizes the parade, which has approximately one hundred entries, including bands, antique cars, and clowns.

TALLAHASSEE

Many art galleries throughout the state have special displays at Christmastime. Typical of those displays is the one by the LeMoyne Art Foundation at 125 North Gadsden Street in the state capital. Each year, as its major fundraiser, LeMoyne has a holiday festival that opens with an elaborate reception, often on Thanksgiving evening, and continues with a display through the end of December. Each show has a theme, such as "Christmas in Florida" or "Anniversaries." The surrounding gardens display an elaborate light show, and the lighting on the front lawn is a major drive-by attraction. For more information, contact the gallery at (904) 222-8800.

TAMPA

One local organization that is often featured at Christmastime is the Community Foundation of Tampa Bay, which has been helping local communities for over ten years. With assets over eighty million dollars, the foundation assists local organizations to make life more bearable and enjoyable for those in the Tampa Bay area.

One of the most generous Tampa residents is Warrick Dunn, running back for the Tampa Bay Buccaneers, who has an annual campaign called "Homes for the Holidays," in which he helps several dozen single mothers and their children move into modest homes of their own by providing a down payment and many furnishings.

Among the local fund-raising programs at Christmastime is the sale of luminarias by the Tampa Palms Ladies Club and New Tampa Junior Woman's Club. The money raised goes for community projects. Luminarias are lighted candles placed in sand-filled paper sacks during the Christmas holidays. The Spanish custom of using lighted candles to guide visitors to their destinations and to bring holiday cheer has become popular in the Tampa area.

WASHINGTON, D.C.

Florida House on Capitol Hill in the nation's capital is a restored nineteenth-century rowhouse that has served Floridians visiting the city since 1973. Staffers provide visitors with information about the city, including tours, historical landmarks, and restaurants. The house serves as a meeting facility and as simply a place to rest. Each year, about ten thousand people visit the house, which is funded through private donations and

A tree with Florida decorations in Florida House, Washington, D.C.
Florida House

governed by a fifty-five-member board of trustees.

For Christmas 1999, a Jacksonville designer, Linn Rainey, was asked to decorate the house with a Florida theme. She decorated a silk Christmas tree with red and gold ornaments, sea biscuits, and sand dollars, crowning the tree with a natural starfish.

After the tree was decorated, the Florida State Society, which consists of displaced Floridians living in the greater Washington area, held its Christmas party at Florida House. The theme was "Come home early for the Holidays . . . to Florida House." For more information about the house, call (202) 546-1555.

WEST PALM BEACH

The Aldrin Planetarium at 4801 Dreher Trail North has a special program during the Christmas season entitled "Star of Wonder." The planetarium uses the show, along with its own "Night Skies Over the Palm Beaches" program, to take visitors back to see the skies during the time of Christ. "Star of Wonder" uses fade-out slides along with a "star globe" to first show visitors how time itself was measured two thousand years ago, prior to the Roman calendar. Then, using Biblical references, the show explores possible dates of the star's appearance. The show then leads visitors onward to show the astronomical events that could have explained the brightness of the Wise Men's star. According to

"Star of Wonder," the Wise Men were probably astronomers in the monarch's court. For further information on hours and prices of admission, call (561) 832-1988.

WINTER HAVEN

The elegant, two-hundred-acre Cypress Gardens tropical theme park has several Christmas-related events each year. From late November through early January, the Garden of Lights holiday festival shows millions of lights throughout the park, including a Star of David and a menorah. "The Legend of Santa Claus" includes many mannequin Santa Clauses—with a written history of each Santa on display—winter scenes, and other holiday treats at the Plantation Emporium. Visitors can also see what is billed as the world's tallest Christmas tree: it's 115 feet tall and has twenty-five thousand lights decorating it.

The annual Poinsettia Festival has three dozen lavishly decorated Christmas trees in partnership with the Greater Winter Haven Junior League Festival of Trees celebration. Festooned with more than forty thousand blooms, the exhibition displays a wide variety of poinsettias, as well as an eight-foot-high waterfall and a miniature Swiss Village railway garden.

In addition to the seasonal exhibits, Cypress Gardens has thousands of tropical flowers along the canals and Lake Eloise, an electric boat ride, water ski shows, hang gliders, circus shows, animal performances and exhibits, and Aquamaids performing a ballet on water.

For more information, call (800) 282-2123 or (941) 324-2111. Web site: www.cypressgardens.com

WINTER PARK

During the past twenty years, over two thousand people have attended the annual lighting of the turn-of-the-twentieth-century Tiffany windows and the Christmas-in-the-Park celebration, held at the beginning of December. The family event is sponsored by the Charles Hosmer Morse Museum of Modern Art in Winter Park. Selected from the Morse's outstanding Tiffany collection, the featured windows set the stage for seasonal favorites from the Bach Festival Choir and Bach Festival Children's Choirs. Throughout December, free concerts attract many to beautiful Central Park, the heart of the district near elegant Park Avenue.

Traditionally, the "Father Christmas and the Christ Child" window is the focal point of the outdoor exhibit. This particular window, designed by *Harper's Weekly* cartoonist Thomas Nast and produced around 1902 by Tiffany Studios incorporates seasonal religious and secular themes. It depicts Father Christmas with the Christ child and, in the background, a candlelit Christmas tree, church spire, mistletoe, and the Three Wise Men following the star to Bethlehem. The other windows, all with religious themes, were produced by Tiffany Glass and Decorating Company for the chapel of the Association Residence in New York City, which was built in the 1880s as a home for elderly, indigent women.

Begun in 1978 by the late Hugh McKean and his wife, Jeannette, to share a part of their rare Tiffany collection with the public in an informal outdoor setting, Christmas-in-the-Park has become a tradition on Park Avenue. Several of the windows are taken to central Florida nursing homes and hospitals after the event. The Morse Mobile Museum, stationed on Park Avenue, invites visitors to browse through the traveling exhibit that has been enjoyed by thousands of people at schools, nursing homes, civic events, and art festivals since it went "on the road" in 1992. For more details, contact the Charles Hosmer Morse Museum of American Art, 445 Park Avenue North. Phone: (407) 645-5311.

Remember that this is only a sample of the many Florida places that have special celebrations at Christmastime. For events scheduled where you live or plan to visit, contact the local chamber of commerce.

BIRD COUNTS, CHRISTMAS TREES, LICENSE TAGS, AND PLACE NAMES

BIRD COUNTS

Every year since 1900, thousands of people have continued an Audubon Society holiday tradition of spending a day between mid-December and the first week of January counting birds to assess the status of early-winter fowl. Volunteers carefully compile records, send them to National Audubon headquarters, and then wait for the results to be published in a book called *Field Notes*. Since 2000, in keeping with the technology boom, birders at any of the more than 1,700 Christmas Bird Counts (CBC) hemisphere-wide have had the option of logging on and sending their results electronically to the BirdSource web site (http:\\birdsource.cornell.edu\) instead of mailing in the results. The web site, a collaborative effort between Audubon and Cornell Laboratory, gives a good summary of the winter distribution patterns of bird species.

The Christmas Bird Count started as a protest against the "Aside hunt," a gruesome tradition in which two teams, or "Asides," competed to see who could shoot the most birds and other small animals in a single day. The slaughter so enraged ornithologist Frank Chapman that he suggested in *Bird-Lore* magazine that conservationists count, rather than shoot, birds on Christmas Day. He and several dozen friends went to twenty-five locations near Englewood, New Jersey, on Christmas Day 1900. What started as a casual protest has turned into the largest wildlife census in the world. Now, more than fifty thousand volunteers in all fifty states, Central and South America, the Caribbean, several Pacific Islands, and every Canadian province participate in the Christmas Bird Count.

In Florida, about two thousand birders take part in this worthwhile pursuit, spending a single day counting birds within a fifteen-mile diameter area (about 177 square miles). The results of those counts help assess the status and health of continental birds, as well as the general state of the environment. Since birds are one of the first groups of animals affected by environmental threats such as pollution and habitat destruction, Christmas Bird Count data provide indispensable information, not only on the long-term health of bird populations but of all living creatures, including ourselves. Counters try to cover as much ground as possible within a twenty-four-hour period.

Two Florida sites (Zellwood/Mt. Dora and Lake Placid) are the only two inland sites east of the Mississippi River to attain 150 species. In 1999, due to unusual circumstances, the Zellwood count reached 174 species, possibly the highest inland count in North America throughout the one-hundred-year history of the CBC.

CHRISTMAS TREES

The Christmas tree, an important part of the holiday for many Americans, has seen a transformation in the kind that most people prefer: the living tree cut from the wild by our colonial ancestors, artificial trees, and those we pick and cut ourselves on tree farms. Even natural trees that we normally buy from local outlets and that are imported from elsewhere, often North Carolina, can now be selected at dozens of tree farms throughout Florida that grow trees suited for the climate of this state.

These cut trees have many advantages. They serve as wildlife habitat while they are growing, increase soil stability and prevent erosion, consume large amounts of carbon dioxide, produce oxygen (each acre of Christmas trees produces enough oxygen to meet the daily oxygen needs of eighteen people), help water seep into the aquifer, and provide beauty to the landscape. After the holidays, disposal crews take away the trees and recycle them. (As organic yard debris, the trees will not be put in landfills.) When the trees decompose and get worked into the ground, they decrease the need for chemical fertilizers. Some trees are chipped into mulch, which is often given free to anyone who wants it.

Florida's tree farms, located throughout the state, average around five acres, although a few have as many as forty acres. Many of those in north Florida were established after freezes in the 1980s destroyed more than two hundred thousand acres of citrus. While many owners of those fields headed to the warmer climate of central and south Florida, others opened up tree farms.

In 1996, Floridians cut down two hundred thousand trees from two hundred "choose 'n cut" farms, netting three million dollars in sales for the owners of the farms. The Florida Christmas Tree Association is an organization of fifty-plus farms that share the latest information about tree farming.

The number of Christmas tree growers has declined over the last several years—not only in Florida but in other states as well—because older farmers are retiring and the younger generation cannot afford to buy land to get started. Christmas tree farming is a lot of hard work, and many younger generation people are not willing to put hard labor into a business they expect to earn little from.

Growing Christmas trees is not as easy as one might think. It takes a lot more than planting some seeds, waiting for the sun and rain to do their work, then selling trees to customers who cut them down and haul them away. Instead, the farmer must care for newly planted trees and later shape and prune them to encourage them to branch more quickly and achieve the bushy appearance we demand in our trees. It takes three to six years for a seedling to grow into a six-foot-tall tree. During that time, farmers must contend with too little or too much sun and rain, and destruction by rodents, insects, disease, hail, or fire. Farmers must treat the ground around the trees, taking out the weeds, vines, and brush that hinder the trees' growth. They grow two or three trees for every tree cut, thus ensuring a continued supply in future years. Farmers also bring in nonnative trees for sale to people who want a tree they are familiar with, such as the Fraser fir.

Typically, farmers plant trees seven feet apart in order to give them enough space to grow. An acre can hold almost a thousand trees. The mild Florida climate allows six- to eight-foot-tall trees to grow in a much shorter time than they would in a colder climate. Unfortunately, Florida's hot weather also causes many problems for tree growers, including pests, diseases, and blights. Probably the worst problem is the Nantucket tip moth, which can kill new growth and quickly devastate a whole farm. The hot summer months are the busiest times for tree farmers as they fight insects and diseases, trim and water the many trees, and perform the many chores necessary to prepare for the onrush of customers after Thanksgiving.

The types of Christmas trees grown in Florida range from the sand pine, red cedar, Leyland cypress, and Arizona cypress in north Florida to Virginia pine and white pine in south Florida. Many Floridians preferred the red cedar because it used to be the only tree that would grow in a

Christmas tree shape and was found easily in the forest. Pine trees do not grow in a Christmas tree shape unless they are trimmed three times a year. Beginning right after Thanksgiving, families drive to nearby tree farms, walk through acres of trees, choose just the right size tree for their home, carefully cut it down, then cart it home. Buying a locally grown tree is good for the environment because less fuel is used in transportation, it enriches Florida's economy, and it's usually cheaper than buying precut trees elsewhere. Cutting such a tree is reminiscent of what our ancestors did a hundred years ago.

Here are a few, helpful hints when you decide to go out and cut your own tree at a tree farm. Wear comfortable clothes and shoes. Most farms supply saws and clippers (though you can bring your own if you want), as well as tree shakers, which are meant to rid the trees of any loose branches or needles. Some farms also have diversions for children such as petting zoos and outdoor trains. Such trees are usually cheaper than those bought at malls or in the cities.

For more information about Christmas trees or nearby tree farms, consult local directories or contact the Florida Christmas Tree Association [1-800-554-TREE (8733)]. And be sure to bring your camera when you go tree hunting.

Decorating a Christmas tree under water.
Florida State Archives

LICENSE TAGS

Throughout Florida, individuals sport license tags that show their fondness for the Christmas season. A person in Apopka has SLEIGH on his tag, while an Ellenton man has SANTA on his. An Orlando driver has S CLAUS, while MRCLAUS appears in Lecanto, and ST NICK is used in Spring Hill.

One man in Bradenton had SANTA on his plate, but he drew in an apostrophe and an S to make it SANTA'S. Before moving to Florida, he had used SANTA BOB on his North Carolina tag, appropriate for someone who played Santa Claus at churches. Other Christmas-related tags in Florida are CLAUS, COMET, CUPID, DANCER, DASHER, DEER, ELF, FROSTY, MZ CLAUS, NOEL, REDNOSE, and RUDOLPH. Personalized plates cost an additional $12 above the normal $27–45 fee.

PLACE NAMES

While Christmas and Fort Christmas are two nearby sites in Orange County, eight other Florida places have "Christmas" in their names: Christmas Bay in Hamilton County, Christmas Cemetery and Christmas Park in Orange County, Christmas Creek in Seminole County, Christmas Island and Christmas Pass in Pinellas County, Christmas Lake in Gilchrist County, and Christmas Point in Miami-Dade County. These are just 10 of the 139 geographical sites in the United States that have "Christmas" in them. Also in the United States are 144 "St. Nicholas," 11 "Santa Claus," 24 "North Pole," 3 "Navidad," and even 3 "Xmas" sites.

CHRISTMAS STORIES
OF FLORIDA

The following stories, both fiction and nonfiction, take place throughout Florida and show different sides of the Sunshine State at Christmastime.

CHRIST WAS BORN IN BETHLEHEM
by Lawrence Dorr

[This story, published here for the first time, is by the author of two collections of short stories: *A Slow, Soft River* (1973) and *A Slight Momentary Affliction* (1987). Born in Hungary to an affluent family, Lawrence Dorr (a pseudonym) became a political refugee after World War II, fled to Austria, became a French Foreign Legionnaire, and emigrated to the United States, where he became a Protestant missionary in Florida, then a ranch hand, and later an editor at the University of Florida. The setting of this story is in north Florida, where the author lives today.]

Clouds the color of a dingy dishrag hid the sun earlier in the morning but by ten o'clock the sky had been transformed into a blue dome cluttered with cumulus resembling melting skyscrapers and mammoth pagodas. December was the time in North Florida when the last of the sun chokes were dug up, all the winter gardens had been planted and some of the pastures seeded with rye. It was the beginning of the twice-a-day grain feeding to keep the horses from losing weight on the poor grass. Since the first frost had turned the grass a warm brown, hay was added to their diet. The old man down at the barn was surrounded by expectant horses, misled by his presence. It was too early for the second feeding. He was only trying to hitch the mower to the tractor.

The last cutting for the year had been at the end of September and the mower had been parked and covered with plastic sheets for the winter. Since then the tractor had only been used to drag trees that had been blown down or struck by lightning into position for the chain saw to provide for next winter's woodpile. It took a year to dry out the wood for the families' fireplaces. Their son and his family lived next to them south of the small woods. Their daughter's family had a house in Gainesville at the edge of the university campus. Most of the heavy work, the cutting and splitting, was done by his son John (his own part was only the lopping off of smaller branches and the chaining and dragging of the tree trunks). His presence and that of John Gray, his ten-year-old grandson, at the operation represented what his mother would have called an *arrière-pensée*.

The ulterior motive in this case was wanting to be working with his boys on the land that he knew was hallowed, land that had been given to him and through him to them for a blessing, a consecration that went beyond title deeds. It could not have come about any other way for a man seven years a Stateless Person, partly in Europe, partly in the United States, a pariah who, in '53 living in Polk County, Florida, couldn't get credit to buy a $126 used roping saddle and so lost a promised job of a fence rider for Lykes Brothers.

Connecting the mower's drive shaft to the tractor's power take-off, he drove in a cotter pin, then climbed up onto the seat. The steering wheel was covered with pipe insulator and electrician's tape, a great improvement on the crumbling plastic underneath. If tractors' ages were counted like dogs', the Ford 4000 and he would be about the same age. He engaged third gear—fourth would pop out at the slightest jarring—and pointed the tractor toward the gate leading to the yard in front of their house because on the way he wanted to pick up his earmuffs: less noise seemed to make the ride smoother. Kicking up their hind legs, the horses began to gallop around the pasture.

Charm still resented being passed by any other horse. She flew over the ground, then braked, almost sliding into the gate. He loved the mare for her beauty, her lovely Arabian-like head, well-proportioned body and her sweetness. She was a 16.2-hands dark-brown Thoroughbred, whose *nom de course*, Thirdonesacharm, had been known around Florida's race tracks before her retirement. It was his daughter-in-law, Anne, who found Charm advertised in a horse magazine and began to correspond with the owners.

When they saw her at a ranch near the Okeechobee swamp, they both liked her but it was Anne who decided to buy her. Two weeks later Charm arrived at their farm in Alachua, dehydrated after her long journey in the August heat. Though she had been separated from her colt for two weeks, her udder was still swollen. He stripped her, thinking that some of his ancestors on his father's side, on their trek from Asia to what was once the ancient Roman province of Pannonia, would have fermented the mare's milk to create an intoxicating drink.

He stopped the tractor, got off, shooed the horses away, opened the gate, climbed back up, drove through, climbed down and closed the gate. Even just a few years ago he wouldn't have noticed all the ups and downs. On the good side of getting old were the sudden illuminations of child-hood mysteries. He understood now why his French mother's family con-sidered his father's family barbarians. They believed the gossip from circa 900 A.D. that Hungarians softened their meat under their saddles and that at weddings Hungarians always ended up smashing their host's wine glasses into the fireplace shouting: "We'll never die."

On his father's side there was resentment toward his mother's family because not only did they dine at 11:00 p.m., by which time their Hungarian cousins were starving, but it was no secret that there was sometimes horsemeat on the menu. What really revulsed them was the knowledge that their French cousins ate horses by choice. This revulsion was never verbalized. It belonged to the same unmentionable category as the knowledge, handed to him at puberty, that Uncle Pali, his father's brother who had never married, allowed the gypsies to live with him in the winter in what the village called "The Castle," and that many of the gypsy children resembled him.

He came out of the house wearing the earmuffs around his neck. The house was flanked by giant hickory trees, two enormous magnolias and some large evergreens beside which a group of small cedars, their friends' former live Christmas trees, looked like jolly Hobbits. Seeing him, Charm neighed. In the beginning of October she had been judged and accredit-ed to the Holsteiner stud book. Since that time, he and Anne had been studying the list of available Holsteiner stallions, their photos, physical attributes, and the placing of their offspring. Narrowing down the choice, they watched videos and finally settled on La Coste, a 17.2-hands dark-brown dressage champion with an eighty-inch hearth girth and nine-inch canon bone. One of La Coste's daughters had won Grand Champion honors as Dressage Sport Horse of the Year.

He climbed back on the tractor, put on his earmuffs and cranked up the engine. From the road only the long roof of his son's house nestled in a hollow was visible. By some optical illusion the trees, azaleas, gardenias, wild yellow and lavender autumn daisies, and even the grass seemed to be reverently marching down toward the house. A mile further on he passed the huge, lightning-damaged oak in the middle of the road and stopped at the corner before turning the tractor onto County Road 241. *Chartres sonne, Chartres t'appelle* his mother used to sing. His destination, the future home of St. Andrew's, two miles away, where he had planned the ground breaking on Christmas Day, had no bells to ring but it called him nevertheless.

The future home consisted of eleven acres, nine of it in planted pine. The property was next to Mount Nebo Church overlooking Interstate 75 toward San Felasco Hammock State Park. He remembered reading an interview years ago in *Time* with a poet who had become the first president of a former French colony in Africa. He didn't know what kind of a president he had made but as a poet writing out of what he called *Negritude* he was fine. As a literary device *Negritude* had disappeared, at least in the United States, but in real estate it still influenced transactions. St. Andrew's small congregation could not have afforded the property if it wasn't for the blessing of its location next to a black church.

He could feel the impatience of the drivers behind him though nobody honked. He had to stop in the middle of the road because the Ford 4000's gearshift didn't work on the fly. The brakes were hardly functional and when he depressed the pedal the tractor slid toward the oncoming traffic. To die on County Road 241 when he had survived the retreat from Kiev fifty-six years ago would be ludicrous, though some might consider it fitting punishment for his hubris in wanting to build a church. But it wasn't pride or arrogance that had made him leave his church home of thirty years. It was his need to worship God in His majesty and Mystery and so to aim to live out the Christian Faith untainted by the world bent on deconstructing Him, a world that looked on all religions in the Age of Aquarius as mere ships to "convey persons to the coast of spiritual knowledge, where faith is no longer required."

He stuck out his left hand, shifted down with the right and made the turn. The sound from the accelerating cars almost blew him out of his seat.

***

He stopped the tractor, removed his earmuffs and got off. Over the susurration of the pines in their ranks was the sound of a swollen, threatening river, the invisible Interstate 75 with its occasional shrieking ambulances. Outside the planted area with its thick, rust-colored floor of pine needles, the grass and weeds were chest high, contrasting with Mount Nebo's well-trimmed cemetery where two men were digging a grave. Their voices and the smell of their cigarettes wafted over on the breeze. Where the bulldozers and front loaders of the big, commercial cemeteries would have conjured up for him images of the Holocaust and the TV news and magazine pictures of the fresh horrors of "ethnic cleansing," the two men with their shovels seemed fitting. They were preparing a final resting place.

He, himself, had wanted to be cremated—his ashes would be less frightening to his grandchildren and easier to deal with—then buried behind their house at the foot of the dogwood that looked like a stage prop for *A Midsummer Night's Dream.* In this there was another of his *arrière-pensées.* He believed that his grave with a modest homemade marker—thirteen-year-old Kate, John Gray and even six-year-old Sara already showed artistic talent—would stop at least two generations from selling the land. But that probably would not happen.

St. Andrew's needed to sell cemetery lots to build a church. As far as his death was concerned, the journey into the unknown did not unduly frighten him. Like Milton's Adam in *Paradise Lost* he accepted life as a gift, an entry into the world that gave him love not only for people but also for the land with its ever-changing shapes and colors, and for the sounds, from the rolling shingle on the Devonshire coast to J.S. Bach, that to him was a never-ending prayer. He waited, though not with the eagerness of a child waiting for his birthday, for his own entry into a larger life of no pain.

He went back to the tractor, put on the earmuffs, cranked up, set the mower lever and started in second gear. The two men looked up from their digging and waved. He waved back, thinking of the gravediggers in *Hamlet* where they talk about Ophelia's suicide without mentioning her name. *If this had not been a gentlewoman, she should have been buried out o' Christian burial.* What had shocked him years ago with racial segregation about to become illegal, was the reading of the angry letters to the editor denouncing the possibility of burying black folk next to white ones. It was then that he had first seen the reality of the theological statement on the fallenness of the human race. In all recorded time only the criteria ever changed by which some were included in the community and some were not.

Mowing in the summer, he always smelled the lovely aroma of freshly cut grass. Now a day before Christmas the dead grass smelled like dust. Cutting across in front of the planted pines he was dazzled by light coming through the tops of the trees creating arched trusses radiating an unearthly glow. There was recognition, but it wasn't Chartres or Exeter or any of the cathedrals he knew. He heard the sound of a Vivaldi mass that always made him cry, not knowing if he was crying because of the beauty of the music or because he knew that God had died for him without first attaching gradations to his worth and usefulness, forgiving his sins, both those he had repented and those he had not.

In '51 he, like Jacob, had been instructed: *Arise, go up to Bethel and dwell there: and make there an altar unto God.* And he too arose, took his wife of fourteen months and their four-week-old baby girl because he had a vision that could not be talked about without being thought peculiar. It was that and the shame he had felt for being able to buy hamburgers anywhere—an "enemy alien" classified World War II ex-tank commander—while some U.S. citizens could not, that made him buy a 1946 maroon Mercury in Ardmore, Pennsylvania for $900, and a grey gabardine suit for $55.99 and head for Florida and the Institute with his wife and baby daughter to be trained as a home missionary. The Institute had been built on 800 acres fifteen miles outside Lime (pop. 1012) between Grantham swamp and Lake Knox, where retired agricultural missionaries instructed trainees in semitropical agriculture for service in Latin America and the destitute rural South.

Mr. Belitt the philanthropist explained at the interview in Philadelphia. The monies for the project were provided by Mr. Belitt, President Truman's Project 4, and some charitable Christians. He should have known that something wasn't quite right when he found out on the evening of their arrival that the Institute consisted of two small houses and a shed and that he, Meg and their baby would be the only people on the place. There was light left on in one of the houses. The door was open. A note on the kitchen table encouraged them to move in and feel at home. The electricity bill would be taken care of by Mr. Belitt. The gas tank with the hand pump was to be used for the tractor to keep the place mowed. They were welcome to use the land for their kitchen garden and small-scale farming projects.

The agreed-on $120 monthly "stipend" was not paid the first six months of their tenure. But it was not all a loss. He did find the "quarters" hidden behind the orange groves out of sight of the tourists. The people in the "quarters" he had come to help invited him to their church to tell them about his escape, his coming to America, and helped him to find temporary jobs in the groves keeping the weeds down with a disc harrow and picking grapefruit. He and his wife both learned to garden in what seemed to them pure sand, raising greens, turnips, radishes, onions, and tomatoes watched over by baby Sibet on her blanket.

When Sibet began to walk, hanging onto walls, chairs, and trees, Mr. Belitt appeared and told them with regret that the Institute had closed. The 800 acres would become the "Heavenly Light Christian Retirement Community." He arranged for them to go to a friend's ranch to look after 200 steers, a Brahman bull, and fifty cows. They would have to build their house with the material provided and would be given the use of a milk cow and $90 a month. The day before they left, the first "Heavenly Light" lot was sold to an elderly couple from Minnesota where the winters "are real cruel."

He finished cutting, shut off the tractor and pulled off his earmuffs. The cooling engine was pinging, then was overwhelmed by the sound of the rushing traffic on I-75. He climbed down from the tractor and walked about on the freshly mowed land. It all looked like satellite photography of the surface of a dead planet where nothing had ever been green. His boots were thickly covered with dust.

The two men at Mount Nebo's cemetery had gone, leaving behind an open grave. Not far from it were the gaudy remains of a recent funeral looking like the pathetic leftovers from a New Year's party: soaked crepe paper streamers, dead flowers in jam jars, already faded ribbons detached from their wreaths lying in the pathways. Clouds of darkness closed over Mount Nebo, closed over him. The clouds swirling overhead looked like smoke. He sniffed the air but there was no smoke in it. Pastures were burned only in the spring, not at the end of December. He felt tired, hopeless. There were only thirty families at St. Andrew's meeting in each other's homes. They needed another $53,000 before the bank would lend them money for the building.

The $23,000 they already had, that had seemed substantial at the last vestry meeting, now looked more like nickels in a child's piggy bank. They needed a thousand dollars a month to pay the mortgage on the land. And there were all the other expenses besides. They couldn't go on allowing their priest to starve. Just as in the presidential elections, where the people with the wherewithal waited for the viable candidate before plunking down their money, so most of the congregation waited to see if St. Andrew's would survive. He shouldn't blame them. They were not told as he had: *make there an altar unto God* and he didn't have the courage to tell them. Old people were watched for signs of senility.

He would have to go home. There were no lights on the tractor. He climbed back on and cranked up. It needed tuning. The sound was as grating on his ears as when somebody bellowed a hymn off key in the pew behind him. He put on his earmuffs wondering what had happened to his understanding of "joyful noise" and his own joyful spirit that could not conceive the possibility of not building St. Andrew's. It was forty-nine years ago when he arose, took his wife and their first child and came down to Florida where he learned what Faith meant for people living in the quarters' shacks whose front doors faced doorless privies a few feet away. Standing in the church door, he was asked time and time again: "Don't you feel blessed living in this beautiful country?" He still remembered their faces and their voices, the only un-hyphenated Americans he knew. Americans who had to sit in the back of buses.

Turning onto County Road 241 he wondered how visible he was to the rushing cars overtaking him. Looking down from the overpass the mad rush of the traffic below made him dizzy. It was getting darker. There would not be ground breaking on Christmas Day. Some of the oncoming cars blinked their headlights.

"No light," he shouted. "I have no light."

He turned off County Road 241 and saw the darker shape of their dying oak tree and beyond it the single light toward which he was driving. It was quite possible that St. Andrew's wouldn't be built in his lifetime. Maybe it would never be built. What mattered was that Christ was born in Bethlehem, that he, sitting on an old tractor, tired and lost would be told again: "Fear not." He only had to run his race and bless God for His blessings of love that had surrounded him and for the land they lived on.

The light from his son's house spilled onto one of the pines transforming the tree into a large Christmas decoration. He wondered if his grandchildren had already hung their stockings on the mantel. His own house was lit up too. He hoped Meg wasn't worried about him being out in the dark without the headlights working. The dogs recognized the sound of the tractor. Chupy's sharp yipping came through the earmuffs.

THE CATFISH THAT TALKED!
by Randolf McCredie

[The following story, reprinted with permission from *Florida Living Magazine* (December 1985), describes a piscatorial tragedy with a happy ending on a Christmas Eve long ago.]

Along main street in downtown Farmdale there were Christmas decorations on every lightpost and on the courthouse square was the most beautiful pine tree in the whole world—at least the people of Farmdale thought so. They had a decorating day on the first Saturday in December and trimmed the tree with gold and silver streamers, colored lights and stars and angels, and there was one big star on the top that outglowed all the rest.

Robert was there with all his friends that day. He ate hot dogs and drank lemonade and sang Christmas carols. It was a happy time and the people all said it would be a fine Christmas, no snow, of course, because Farmdale was in north Florida, but it might be warm enough to go swimming, or on the other hand, it could be cold enough for frost or even ice on the horse trough at the farm.

Despite the time of year, Robert was not happy.

His mother noticed the air of gloom that seemed to hover around his face like some kind of cloud and she said, "Robert, are you ill? Are you coming down with a cold right here at Christmas?"

"I don't like Christmas," Robert said heatedly. "You save your money all year and then you have to go buy presents for everybody."

"Why, Robert, that's selfish," his mother said. "This is Christmas. Everybody gives presents at Christmas. This is the time for giving."

"I don't care," Robert answered. "I've got enough money to buy that electric train at Simmons Hardware and now I have to use all the money just because it's Christmas."

By this time Robert's mother was becoming angry with her son. "I think you'd better go to your room and think about this," she said. "Just suppose everybody decided not to give you anything for Christmas."

"I don't care," Robert said as he left the room. "Anyway, Joey's not going to give me a present. He said he's broke this year."

With that, he ran up to his room.

The next morning he still felt there was something wrong about saving money all year and then having to spend it on other people. "It's my money," he thought. "I should be able to spend it on myself."

After breakfast, he went down to the fish pond to tell his troubles to his catfish friend, Jerry.

Jerry saw him coming and popped his head above the water near his favorite rock.

"It's a beautiful day, and Christmas is coming next week," he said to Robert.

"It's not a beautiful day," Robert said crossly, "and I wish Christmas wouldn't come. Then I could spend my money on an electric train."

"Oh ho," said the catfish, ducking his head under water to get a gulp of oxygen before continuing. "What have we here? A boy who doesn't like Christmas? I never heard of such a thing!"

"That's fine for you to say," said Robert. "You're just a catfish and you don't know anything about Christmas. You don't have to give your things away to others."

The catfish was silent for what seemed like a long time, slowing fanning his tail back and forth in the clear water. Finally, he said, "I think it's time I told you a true story. And it's about a catfish who gave everything he had to others."

"Aw, catfish don't have anything to give away," Robert said sarcastically.

"You know Mr. Miller, the man who does chores around the barn for your father?" the catfish asked.

"Mr. Miller who was born deaf?" Robert asked. "Is that the man you're talking about?"

"That's the man," said Jerry, "but he wasn't born deaf. That's what he says. What really happened is that he lost his hearing when he was a boy playing with dynamite. He used to throw dynamite into this pond to kill a lot of fish at one time."

"Dynamite in this pond," Robert frowned. "I never heard of that, and why didn't it kill you and all the other catfish?"

"It happened a long time ago, before I was born," Jerry explained. "And many members of our family were killed. My father told me the story. My grandfather was the biggest catfish in this pond, wise and kind and gentle. The fish had elected him president of our council—and then a terrible thing happened."

"How could anything terrible happen in this ole pond?" Robert asked. "Unless it was the dynamite."

"It was the dynamite," said Jerry. "My grandfather saw young Miller coming to the pond. He saw him light the fuse and throw the stick into the pond. Then, even though he was old, he darted for the stick, took it in his mouth and started for the far end of the pond. At the same time he signaled for all the other fish to swim down to the other end."

"What happened then?" Robert wanted to know.

"The dynamite went off and grandfather was blown to bits. You see, he gave everything he had for the other fish in the pond. And it was Christmas Eve."

Jerry blinked his eyes rapidly to keep from crying at the thought of such a tragedy on Christmas Eve. "My father said that year the pond had a bad Christmas."

"What happened to Mr. Miller?" Robert asked.

"He gathered up the dead fish and went away, but he got caught later when a stick of dynamite went off too soon at another pond. It went off before he could throw it very far and he lost his hearing."

That night at the supper table, Robert told his mother, "After school tomorrow I'm going to buy Joey a Christmas present. I don't care if he can't buy me one this year."

Robert's mother wondered what had changed her son's mind about Christmas, but she was happy that he had decided on his own that giving at Christmas and all year was more important than receiving.

ALMOST A CHRISTMAS BRIDE
by Maxine S. Nicholson

[The following story, reprinted with permission from *Florida Living Magazine* (December 1987), features the towns of Dunnellon, Homosassa, Crystal River, and Inverness, which are all relatively close today but didn't seem so back in the days before superhighways.]

I always told my children, or anyone else who asked, that their father and I were married on Christmas Day. We weren't, but we tried.

I had dreams about my wedding. I would float down our staircase in my mother's 24-year-old satin and lace wedding dress, a sheath of orange blossoms on my arm. There in our living room, at the foot of the stairs, L.P. would be waiting. He would put out his arm and I would take it. We would move gracefully together to the strains of the "Wedding March." No one in our family played, but we did have an old upright piano, out of tune now and untouched except for dusting since we girls used to bang on it.

The minister (I had to have a minister) would be standing behind the rose-colored lamp on the study table.

We had picked out the minister at Easter when L.P. and I had gone to his church in Dunnellon. He was young, his voice musical. He did not shout or pound the lectern as our preacher did.

L.P. had whispered, "That's the minister we'll have to marry us."

I had agreed.

When I told Mother I wanted orange blossoms at my wedding, which she was sure was years away, she had frowned.

"What a waste of oranges."

We didn't have a single orange tree, but my uncle had groves of them, and I had been sure he would let me pick big bouquets of blossoms for my wedding.

So much for dreams. Now we were riding around on Christmas afternoon, trying to decide how we would ever persuade Mother to let us marry that evening.

When I had broached the subject back in August, Mother had been ready for me.

"It isn't that I object to L.P. Before you marry, you need to have an education. None of your sisters had the chance to go to college as you do."

It was true. My uncle, the one with the orange groves, was willing to send me to college. If I hadn't fallen in love with L.P., I'd have jumped at the chance.

"Besides," Mother continued, setting her lips in a thin, straight line, "L.P. doesn't have a steady job."

She said a great deal more. Her lectures could last for hours. I didn't have the courage to tell her L.P. had already bought my wedding ring.

The ring was in L.P.'s pocket on Christmas Day. I bit my fingernails trying to figure a way to get Mother's consent for me to quit college after three months to become L.P.'s bride. L.P. had a steady job now, but I was still under age (which at that time was 21), and Mother had to be reckoned with. Besides, I did want to be married by a minister in the home where I had been born.

We were stumped.

"What about Paul?" I asked.

Paul was L.P.'s cousin. All I knew about him was that he had gone with L.P.'s brother and his wife, my best friend, to talk her mother into letting them marry the year before.

So we began our quest to have a Christmas wedding. It was a long time ago, but we didn't ride in a horse and buggy, as someone (I think it was a grandchild) suggested. Our transportation this frosty afternoon was an old secondhand Chevrolet with no heater and windows that didn't quite roll up.

Eighteen miles to Dunnellon. Paul wasn't home.

"He's on the Mullet Special and staying in Homosassa," his wife explained. Paul was a railroad engineer.

We drove to Homosassa.

Eighteen miles back to Crystal River. Ten more miles to Homosassa. Are you keeping track?

We arrived back in Crystal River with Paul just as the sun was setting.

Mother was not happy to meet Paul, not when she found out his mission.

Paul was a short, red-faced man. He was tongue-tied.

Mother was a dumpy little woman with prematurely white hair and a ready smile. Only tonight she wasn't smiling.

Paul stuttered and stammered. Mama boiled. She didn't say a word. She just stood there on the front porch, her lips pressed into a thin, straight line, her jaw tight.

I stood transfixed, staring at my gentle, quiet mother, so seldom had I seen her angry, never had I heard her raise her voice.

Paul stammered on. I didn't hear what he was saying. After what seemed hours, Mother turned to L.P. "I want to speak to you alone," she said. And she marched him to the back of the house.

Later, I learned what was said.

She told him I wasn't mature enough for marriage. She told him I was lazy.

"I'll get her out of that," he said. She told him I didn't know how to keep house, that I couldn't cook.

"I'll teach her," he said.

She told him I had a bad temper.

Never had a man been so informed of his bride's shortcomings. At last, having run out of breath, or because she couldn't think of another fault to lay at my feet, Mother said, "Very well. Remember, I didn't ask you to marry her. When things go wrong, don't think you can bring her back."

With that she strode back to the front porch where Paul and I stood staring at each other.

It was my turn.

When we were in her bedroom, Mother was her gentle, pleading self.

"I did so want you to have an education. It's not that I object to L.P. He will always work, but you need to be prepared in case you ever have to support yourself."

I listened.

Finally, she asked, "If you and L.P. were on a desert island, starving, and had only one crust of bread, would you give him half?"

I thought about it. I had never been truly hungry, knew nothing of starvation. I felt I could manage on half and was thankful she didn't ask me if I would give him the whole slice.

I said, "Yes."

"It's your decision. Remember though, when you leave you can't come back."

I believed her.

Ten miles in the dark to Homosassa to deposit Paul.

We had invited him to stay for the wedding, but he had declined. I suspect he had had enough of us for one night.

Ten miles back to Crystal River.

Two middle-aged ladies, winter visitors, had dropped in to see what a Southern Christmas was like. When they learned there was to be a wedding, they decided to stay on for that.

Mother refused to go with us for the marriage license. She was gracious. She had guests.

. Nineteen miles to Inverness, the county seat. Judge May was at home, in his robe and slippers. He didn't ask my age. He didn't need to.

"Where is your mother, Maxine?" he asked, peering over his glasses at me.

"At home," I stammered.

"Go back and have her sign these papers." He looked hard at me. "It had better be her signature. I know her handwriting."

Nineteen miles back to Crystal River. Nineteen miles back to Inverness with Mother's signature.

It was getting late.

Now all we had to do was inform the minister that we were hauling him out of his warm bed on Christmas night to have the honor of marrying two people he didn't even know.

Eighteen miles from Inverness to Dunnellon to wake the preacher.

Eighteen miles back to Crystal River. Oh, but it was worth it!

I floated down the stairway in my best blue crepe suit, the one with the wide pink satin brocade collar and cuffs. Mother wouldn't let me wear her wedding dress; the satin was so old it was falling to pieces.

"If you had let me know soon enough, we could have remade it with new satin," she said.

L.P. waited for me now at the foot of the stairs, his brown hair gleaming in the light like pine needles on the forest floor when the sun strikes them, his brown eyes twinkling, his dimples just showing.

He took my hand and we marched across the sitting room floor to the strains of the "Wedding March." One of our guests was playing on our old out-of-tune piano in the cold parlor across the hall. The minister was waiting behind the study table with its rose-colored lamp.

And so we were married. I didn't have orange blossoms, except the tiny ones engraved on my wedding band. They are gone now, worn away with 50 years of washing and sweeping and mopping floors, and diapers and babies, children, grandchildren, and great-grandchildren. But the ring is still on my finger where L.P. placed it with trembling hands that night so long ago. Gold and love wear well.

The minister signed the marriage license. He dated it.

The Christmas tree with its colored lights glittered in the corner. Its spicy cedar scent filled the air, but . . . it was four o'clock in the morning on December 26. We tried.

A MERRY FLORIDA CHRISTMAS
by Maxine S. Nicholson

[The following description of an early Christmas, reprinted with permission from *Florida Living Magazine* (December 1986), tells what such celebrations were like many years ago.]

I was born and brought up in Crystal River on the west coast of North Central Florida when it was an out-of-the way fishing village.

At that time we had a new red brick schoolhouse, three churches, Baptist, Methodist and Presbyterian, a cedar mill, a crate mill and two or three fish houses. We boasted of 1,000 inhabitants, and I suppose there were, if you counted the cats and dogs, and everybody knew each other's cat and dog, by name.

We had storms sometimes during the hurricane seasons when the wind would howl and snatch the roots of the huge oaks in our front yard out of the ground. Sometimes the wind wrestled long enough to hold the tides in and flood the town.

The men would fire guns in the middle of the night to warn people in the low-lying areas to seek higher ground. Everybody too young to be married donned bathing suits and paddled rowboats up and down the streets. All the stores had a baptism of water and mud; all the children were lined up for typhoid shots.

In the winter during the coldest months we had frost and ice-crusted buckets, but never, never snow.

No snow on Christmas?

It couldn't have mattered less to us as we chugged over the deep sand ruts in Daddy's Model-T truck. Ruth sat importantly in the front seat with Gladys wedged between her and Daddy, who was driving. Lucy and I bounced merrily in the truck bed, safely latched behind the chicken wire sides Daddy had built to enclose his hunting dogs.

We sang "Jingle Bells," off key, at the top of our lungs. We had never seen a sleigh, except in pictures, and had no idea what a bobtail was. We were acquainted with horses—distantly. Snow was a mysterious white substance we had read about in books and seen pictures of on post cards: probably like cotton or the white sand in the ruts. But regardless of the songs we sang and the Christmas cards, it wasn't necessary to have snow to have a merry Christmas.

Daddy stopped the truck at Cedar Grove and we scurried through the oaks and other hardwoods searching for the perfect cedar for our Christmas tree.

We scampered about shouting, "This one, Daddy!"

But each, on close examination, had some flaw, until at last Ruth discovered the most symmetrical tree.

When it was cut and brought home, Daddy had to perform more surgery to make it fit the 12-foot ceilings in our parlor. When at last it stood beautiful, glistening, aromatic, with the library table and the piano shoved off in corners to make room for it, we began to decorate.

We had no lights, no candles. We strung yards and yards of green and red ropes, glistening tinsel, fastened fragile glass ornaments onto branches, tied on white paper snowflakes we had learned to make in school. At the very topmost branch in the place of honor, we hung the Christmas angel. Then the parlor door was closed and locked until Christmas morning.

Christmas services at the church brought us back to the true meaning of Christmas. We marched the half block through a frosty night in our Sunday best to the pealing of church bells, up the broad steps of the white wooden edifice, happy for once to sit on the hard wooden benches, to sing carol after carol and to listen to Mr. Harvey Edwards, our Sunday School superintendent, read the beautiful nativity passage from the large Bible on the lectern.

Mary, Joseph and the Baby, the wise men and shepherds occupied the platform. The choir stall housed a Christmas tree, tall, and even more beautiful than the one shut up in our parlor. On the branches of the tree hung packages. Old Santa called out to each child by name to come forward and claim his or her gift.

If an unexpected child or two appeared, Santa would scramble around under the tree, find a package that had "lost" its tag and beg someone to tell him the name of the child it belonged to. We left the church, merry, singing carols and hugging our small gifts.

Almost by the time we could talk, we knew "The Night Before Christmas" by heart, but not only did we have no snow, we didn't have a chimney.

Even our vivid imaginations could not visualize Santa climbing through our stovepipes into our wood heater, but with the faith of the very young, we hung our stockings fastened with a large safety pin on the foot of our iron bedsteads.

Sure enough, next morning we would find them stuffed with apples, oranges, nuts, and candy and in the toe a tiny china doll no bigger than your thumbnail, or maybe a dozen pennies.

Clasping our new treasures, we ran barefoot over the icy floors, down the stairs, through the sitting room, across the hall to the parlor. The door was unlocked at last; the Christmas tree was now resplendent with presents.

CHRISTMAS IN OCALA
by Joan Savage Olson

[This story, reprinted from *Florida Living Magazine* (December 1987) takes place in the small town of Candler and the city of Ocala.]

Daddy had built the little house in Candler with green lumber. The wide boards ran up and down and where these boards joined he nailed narrower boards. Thus, when the wide green boards shrunk we would not have cracks in our house.

There were three rooms in our house. One was a large combination bedroom and sitting room where Mother and Daddy and my new baby sister and I slept. The other smaller bedroom was the boys' room—Ulmer, Marion and Charlie, when Charlie was home but he was staying in Ocala in Grandfather's house (Savage House) going to school. There was no high school in Candler. Charlie worked on weekends for money so that he could buy his groceries during the week.

The largest and most cheerful room was the big airy kitchen with the huge black cookstove with the warming oven and the big oven for baking and the huge table, which Daddy had made and which was laden with food, good homemade bread, home-grown meat, and vegetables. At one side of the kitchen next to the wall were the barrels—flour, cornmeal, sugar, rice and grits. We were a long way from the stores and Daddy wanted us to have all the essential staples.

Ulmer and I played outside among the new grown pine saplings, climbing them and swinging on them as they were pulled over to the ground by our weight. We were flying just like the birds. It was wonderful.

When Marion came home from the school in Candler, he would pull me around the yard in a contraption he had made from two old buggy wheels and a handle. He made slingshots for Ulmer and they practiced target shooting with them. I wanted a slingshot too, but Marion thought I was too little. I pleaded and he told me that if I could pull the rubberband on his slingshot he would make one for me. I tried to pull the band and the pebble shot fell almost at my feet, but nevertheless Marion promised to make a slingshot for me when he returned from hunting the next day.

That night one of Marion's friends came to spend the night as they were leaving for hunting across the sawgrass near Candler. Daddy had to go to Ocala that day on business and Charlie went with him. As Daddy was leaving, he told Marion and his friend, Johnnie, not to load their guns until they got across the sawgrass.

A tragic hunting accident occurred that day about noon and Marion was instantly killed.

Shortly after this, Daddy's sawmill burned to the ground. There was no insurance. My parents were devastated with grief and loss.

We moved to Ocala and lived in Grandfather Savage's house. Mother was ill and my grandparents took my baby sister to Lake Harris, where they were living, to care for her during this time.

The winter of 1917 was cold in Ocala. Daddy was working in Marshall Swamp on the Ocklawaha River, cutting the big trees and putting together a raft. The mules hauled these trees to the river where Daddy fastened them together for the raft. This should have been the work for a crew of men but Daddy had no money to pay the "hands," so with the help of the mules, he did this himself. He would attach the raft to a motor boat and go down the Ocklawaha to where it joins the St. Johns River and from there on to Jacksonville the current would float and carry the raft. There Daddy hoped to sell the raft.

I was in the first grade at Ocala Primary School. I liked school and enjoyed my walk of a mile each day to and from school. Mother was sick and that made me sad. It was very cold, and we had fuel only for the cook stove.

In school we were making pretty things for Christmas, pictures and posters and small gifts and some woven mats. At reading time the teacher told us stories of Christmas. We became more excited each day as Christmas neared.

We children talked of what we wanted for Christmas. I wrote a letter to Santa Claus and mailed it in the nearest post office box at the corner of High Street and Ocklawaha Avenue. I asked Santa for skates. My doll from last year's Christmas was still good and I loved her and liked to play with her. Now I wanted skates and I felt sure Santa would bring them to me. I tried especially hard to be good.

The Friday afternoon before Christmas holidays began, our class had a program with the second and third grades singing and reciting Christmas songs and poems. The school Christmas tree was so pretty. We had decorated the tree with chains and stars and many other things we had made in school. The teacher brought the tinsel, which was shiny and bright.

Our teacher gave a pencil to each of us. We were delighted with this as we were not allowed to take our school pencils home.

I hurriedly walked and soon came to the mailbox—Santa Claus post office box—and I made my last turn for home. Life was beautiful and simple.

Ulmer had arrived home before me as he could walk faster. We told Mother of our school program as we tidied her room a bit. Then I washed the dishes in cold water. The morning fire had long gone out so the water in the kettle was cold. I did this job each day. I put the dishpan on a low table and used a low stool for this task. While I washed dishes, Ulmer brought in wood for the supper fire and morning fire for breakfast.

Our chores done, Ulmer and I went out to play in the trees until it was dark. We waited for Charlie to come home from the post office. He would cook our supper for us. We watched the beautiful winter sky with its gorgeous golden, reddish hues.

At suppertime Charlie told us about the Christmas tree program and party Ocala might have for the girls and boys. We told him about our school party.

Charlie was 18 years old, not as old as Grandfather, but three times my age!

The next night Charlie came home with the wonderful news that Ocala was really and truly honest to goodness going to have the Christmas tree and gifts for the kids of Ocala.

But how would we go? Ulmer could go downtown in the daytime and take me with him, but he could not go at night alone and I could not go downtown at all alone. Mother was sick and could not take us, so what could we do? Mother helped us work it out.

Since Ulmer could go downtown alone, he could go to the post office and wait there for Charlie to get off from work. During the Christmas season Charlie never knew when he would get off from work as he was a special delivery carrier. Ulmer was to wait in the lobby and sit on the stairs which led to the upper floor. Mother cautioned him to be still and quiet and not to disturb anyone. Then when Charlie got off from work they would go to the Christmas tree party. That was fine for Ulmer, but what about me? My situation was different. Charlie could not have two kids at the post office and Mother could not take me.

We all hoped Daddy would come home from the swamp for Christmas. He usually walked the ten miles from the river to Ocala as the mules which hauled the big trees to the river needed their rest. The day of the Ocala Christmas party arrived. Ulmer went to the post office that afternoon to wait for Charlie. Would Daddy come home? I knew he would come home for Christmas if possible.

In the midafternoon Mother let me build a fire in the cookstove with kindling Ulmer brought in. I had the damper wide open as I lit the kindling, heeding Mother's warning to be careful when using matches. I put the zinc tub on the stove and used a small pot to fill the tub about two-thirds full with water. The kindling in the stove was burning well and the stove was hot. I put some larger slow-burning hickory and oak on the fire and when that was going well I shut down the damper. The water would stay warm for Daddy's bath. Then I got out his clean clothes and put them on a chair in the kitchen. I wanted everything ready so we could go to the Christmas tree party.

Now it was getting dark and I thought Daddy might not get home in time. Mother told me not to expect it because something might have happened to prevent Daddy coming home. But I believed he would come. I knew he would come! It was Christmas Eve and I wanted my Daddy home.

It was dark now but I had not given up hope. Then I heard Daddy's footsteps. I ran to the door, opened it and Daddy hugged and kissed me and threw me high in the air above his head and caught me. I hurriedly told him of the plan. Mother corroborated this. Daddy bathed and dressed as quickly as possible and we started downtown to the Christmas tree party. I talked incessantly about our school party and so many other things as I tripped gaily along to the Christmas tree.

Oh, there it was! In front of the Ocala House across from the bandstand on the courthouse square. Lines were roped off for the children to come forward for their gifts from Santa. But there was no line! I was terrified that Santa would not have a gift left for me as I went to greet him. "Ho! Ho!" Santa greeted me, in his bright red suit and white beard. "Let's see what we can find for you." He found a red bag of candy in one box and then an apple and in another box he found an orange. Oh, wonder of wonders! Candy, an apple and an orange. The bounty of the universe had surely fallen on me!

I told Santa we were going to the hardware store on the corner of Broadway and Magnolia to try on skates so they would fit right and would he please get those exact skates and bring them to my house for Christmas. Santa nodded approval. That was our next stop. I tried on the skates and Daddy told the clerk to put my name on them as Santa was going to pick them up and they must be those special skates. Daddy bought candy and nuts for Mother.

After that Daddy and I walked home in the brisk Florida Christmas Eve. The sky was twinkling with stars, and the pungent scent of burning wood in the fireplaces and stoves was tantalizingly sweet. When we arrived home, I rushed in to tell Mother about the party and gifts, which I shared with her.

It was a long time before I fell asleep that night. I was almost too happy to sleep.

I awakened Christmas morning tingling with anticipation. There was a nice food smell coming from the kitchen. Daddy was cooking breakfast and singing. We had grits, sausage and eggs and flapjacks. Daddy flipped these over by tossing them into the air and they fell back into the pan on the other side. What a sumptuous breakfast. But best of all Mother was better and ate breakfast at the table with us.

Santa brought my skates—my special skates—and I had gone to the Christmas tree party. I was so happy I thought my body could not hold all my happiness and that I might burst.

After breakfast Charlie and I went to the paved sidewalk on Adams Street about a block from Savage House. Charlie fitted my skates on my shoes for me and adjusted the toe pieces and straps around my ankles. He helped me to my feet and held my hand while I skated a little. Charlie was afraid I would fall, but I had no fear and was soon skating a little.

By the time the Christmas holidays were over, I skated to school.

Ah! Happy, happy childhood!

CHRISTMAS AT CROSS CREEK
by Marjorie Kinnan Rawlings

[This nonfiction piece by one of Florida's most famous writers, originally published in *American Cookery* (December 1942), describes the Christmas of 1928, soon after Rawlings moved to the small town of Cross Creek.]

It seemed to me that my first Christmas at Cross Creek would break my heart. I knew better than to expect snow on Christmas Eve. It was unreasonable to be outraged by a temperature of 75 degrees, hot blazing sunshine and red birds singing lustily instead of Christmas carolers. A half, or is it a fourth, of the world is warm at Christmas time. I had moved to the sub-tropics, and the lush life had become my life. Yet the bland air infuriated me. In pique, I built a great roaring log fire in the living room of the old Florida farmhouse—and was obliged to fling wide all doors and windows. But as I set the table on the sunny veranda for Christmas dinner, the yellow flames in the open fireplace were comforting.

I was further appalled when, at one o'clock, shortly before I was ready to serve dinner, two rural neighbors named Moe and Whitey appeared in clean blue jeans and blue shirts for a visit. I hinted that the family dinner was ready and their expressions grew polite and also acquiescent. Why didn't they go home? In desperation, I invited them to have dinner with us. To my horror, they accepted. The wreck of the day was complete.

Since then, I have come to love the lazy and casual Florida backwoods Christmas. The function of all such festive days is to give us a sense of cozy hominess, of belonging to something stable and lovely. And it is all a matter of the things to which one is accustomed. Now that Cross Creek is "home," I should be as infuriated as on that first Christmas day, if snow fell, and sparrows pecked at ice. The red bird's song is the accepted Christmas paean. And miracle of miracles, we have in abundance our own holly and mistletoe. The Christmas tree is not a symbol in Cracker Florida, but every family breaks mistletoe to hang above the fireplace, and cuts a great bough of holly to stand upright, bright with red berries, in a corner of the pine cabin.

The men, and some of the women, consider Christmas as one of the great days for hunting. That, too, goes back to something solid and important, when men made their living, pioneer fashion, in the woods. The relation of man to nature continues. It is the mode to cook for

Christmas dinner whatever the men bring down with their guns. That, too, is stable and is good. I myself consider that game, quail, dove, rabbit, turkey, or venison, is better when aged a bit in the icebox. But in the old days there were no iceboxes, and folks lived and ate from day to day and from meal to meal. And having partaken of Christmas dinner in the Big Scrub and in other remote places, I cannot say that fresh-killed meat is any the less delicious. The men have brought it in and the women have cooked it, and an old, good way of life is maintained. The beverage is likely to be Florida "corn," or moonshine liquor, with, for the more delicate or puritanical women, home-made Scuppernong or blackberry or elderberry wine.

What the men hunt for Christmas dinner depends on what game frequents their locale. In the Big Scrub, in Gulf Hammock, in the Florida Everglades, it is wild turkey or deer. At Cross Creek it is quail or dove or rabbit or wild ducks. On Christmas morning, after the cows have been milked, the wood for kitchen range and fireplaces brought in, "Little Will," the colored grove man, asks for permission to hunt. I understand why the morning chores have been done so early and so efficiently. Permission is given. This last year, Little Will was gone exactly one hour. He came in with five wild Mallard ducks for Christmas dinner at the tenant house. I questioned him. All through the fall, he had observed, bringing in the cows from the lakeside hammock, that a flock of wild Mallards was "using" in a little cove on Cross Creek. All Little Will had to do was crouch on the bank and bring down his Christmas dinner. I was, frankly, jealous, having gone to great trouble in far places to shoot wild ducks. Little Will had never mentioned to me the flock at my back door. He was assuring his own Christmas, and quite rightly.

Turkey is not necessarily the main Christmas dish in rural Florida. Unless one can have wild turkey, so many other wild meats are available and more than acceptable. Little Will's acquisition of wild ducks put an idea in my own head. For some years I have had my own flock of Mallard ducks. They were raised originally from a setting of eggs from the Carolina marshes hatched under one of my game hens. The flock grew in size, until some years I have had as many as seventy ducks. They live and range freely, never leave the orange grove, and their meat is especially flavorsome because of their diet of mash, scratch feed and skimmed milk in addition to their natural foods of greens, frogs and insects. They are fatter and in flavor much sweeter than truly wild ducks, yet less fat and greasy and insipid than market domestic ducks. While I still sometimes have turkey for Christmas dinner, I am more than likely to have my Mallard ducks. The day makes a suitable occasion for cutting down their inordinate and expensive numbers. The flock costs as much to feed as two or three mules!

Here is my menu for Christmas duck dinner at Cross Creek:

Baked sherried grapefruit
Roast duck
Wild rice
Giblet gravy
Tiny cornmeal muffins
Braised white onions
Sweet potatoes in orange baskets
Crisp celery
Tart jelly—currant, wild grape or wild plum
Green salad
Dry red wine, Burgundy or claret
Tangerine sherbet

RECIPES

BAKED SHERRIED GRAPEFRUIT

Cut grapefruit in halves and separate sections as for breakfast serving, without cutting sections entirely through. Turn upside down to drain off excess juice. Dot grapefruit with butter, brown sugar (or honey) butter and powdered clove. Fill centers with sherry. Brown under broiler or in very hot oven.

ROAST DUCK

In using wild duck, I do not make the conventional stuffing of onion or celery or apple. I dress the ducks whole, salt and pepper them, and place them breast side up in a tightly covered roasting pan with an inch of hot water in the pan. The oven is at 450° F. for the first 15 minutes. Then I reduce the heat to 350° F. Young ducks will roast in little over one hour. For older ducks, I allow from 2 to 3 hours. They should be basted every 15 minutes with the liquid in the pan. I allow ½ duck per person. An occasional greedy or hungry guest will eat a whole duck but is not encouraged. I boil the giblets in hot water until tender, put through the meat grinder, and add to the gravy, which is made by adding 2 to 4 table-spoons of flour, salt and pepper, to the fat in the roasting pan.

WILD RICE

Wild rice expands in cooking more than white rice, and a half-cup serves where a whole cup of white rice is needed. Boil 20 minutes in salted water, or until tender, drain, pour hot water over it; drain and let stand in a colander over hot water 5 to 10 minutes.

CORNMEAL MUFFINS

1¼ cups flour
¼ cup cornmeal
½ teaspoon salt
4 teaspoons baking powder
¼ cup milk
1 egg
¼ cup melted butter or vegetable shortening

Sift together dry ingredients. Add milk, then beaten egg, then melted shortening. Bake in tiny muffin pans in a hot oven (425° F.). Makes about 20 small muffins.

BRAISED ONIONS

Peel small to medium white onions and cook them whole in a small quantity of salted water. Allow 4 small onions or 2 or 3 medium ones per person. Cook until extremely tender, allowing all the water to boil away. Add 1 tablespoon butter and 1 teaspoon sugar for every 4 to 6 onions. Simmer until onions are well browned, turning often. Serve with the brown juice.

TANGERINE SHERBET

1 cup sugar
1½ cups water
Grated rind of 4 tangerines
4 cups tangerine juice
Juice of 1 or 2 lemons

Boil sugar and water 10 minutes. Add the grated tangerine rind to syrup while hot. Let cool slightly and add tangerine juice and lemon juice. Taste for sweetness and acidity, as the tangerines vary. Chill thoroughly, strain and freeze.

A TURKEY FOR ALL SEASONS
by Virginia T. Stephens

[The following story, reprinted with permission from *Florida Living Magazine* (December 1987), is about a turkey that may have thought he was a dog.]

"Wake up, Sissy," Ma shouted. "Get yourself out to the garden in a hurry and chase that dang turkey out of my vegetables. Then you find out how he got in there and fix the fence so it don't happen again!" I could tell that Ma was hopping mad. The garden was more than a hobby. It was a necessity now that we were alone and pinching our pennies.

It was not Pa's intention when he took the temporary job in Millville to desert us. Actually, Millville was less than a hundred miles away, and Pa's second-hand Model A Ford was in good condition even though the roads were not. He wanted to take Ma and me with him, but she flatly refused to budge from our half-acre homestead on the edge of our small town in North Florida.

Ma assured Pa we'd be safe as long as Tige was there to protect us. Tige was Ma's part German shepherd dog that was several years older than me. Tige's best friend was Old Baldy, a turkey we owned because a couple of years before I'd persuaded Ma to add a turkey egg I'd been given to a setting of hen's eggs.

"Old Baldy thinks he's a dog," Pa said as he watched them playing last summer. Old Baldy teased Tige all the time and often ate his food, especially the hoe-cakes Ma cooked when the corn meal got old and webby.

"He's about as big as Tige," I agreed. "That's because he eats like a horse," Ma put in. "He sure don't act kin to the chickens. He just struts around all the time like he owns the place. Sissy, I do wish you'd make him stop pestering Tige."

It was the middle of the Great Depression, and Pa took the job even though it meant being away from home and having to pay board as well as travel costs to and from Millville. He said that between Ma's green thumb and my sales ability we'd make it until times got better and he could find a job at home.

Pa had built me a wagon which Ma and I loaded with her produce every Saturday morning. I pulled it down to the corner of the next block and sold vegetables to the passers-by, mostly neighbors who didn't have gardens. I always took Tige along on his rope. He stayed beside me, scratching or napping while I sold whatever was in season.

The pecans had started falling and it looked like there was going to be a bumper crop. If we could just keep the Baxter boys from climbing the wire fence and stealing our pecans, we'd have enough money from the pecans to pay our taxes.

Pa came home on weekends until his car broke down. He had to save up to get it repaired, so we didn't see him for over a month. During that time Tige got sick and died. Ma blotted her eyes on her apron and the two of us dragged his body to a hole Ma had dug under the big oak tree. Both of us cried as we covered him with dirt.

The Saturday after we buried Tige, I could hardly make myself go down to the corner. It wouldn't be the same without Tige. But as Ma and I loaded the wagon, Old Baldy kept coming close to me and gobbling softly. He led me to the back porch where Tige's old collar and rope hung from a nail on the pump shelf. He pecked at it till it came off its hook.

"Ma," I said, "look at Old Baldy. I think he wants me to put Tige's collar on him."

"Maybe he wants to go to the corner with you like Tige did," she answered.

That was exactly what Old Baldy wanted. I slipped the collar over his head and it dropped down around his breast. He strutted ahead of me just as he'd seen Tige do every Saturday for the past year. I held the rope with one hand and pulled the wagon with the other. When we reached our destination, I looped the end of the rope around a bush while Old Baldy looked around the area, scratching in the grass for bugs and clucking to warn me when someone approached. I told him to be quiet or he'd scare away the customers.

"Sure was sorry to hear about your dog dyin', Sissy," Mrs. Pembroke said. Our neighbors had known Tige all his life, and they knew how much protection he was with Pa away.

"Thankee, Ma'am," I answered politely. "Whatcha askin' for the turkey?" she inquired.

"Oh, he ain't for sale. He just come along to keep me company. Guess he knowed I'd be missin' Tige."

"Well, he sure is a nice fat bird. He'd make a fine Christmas dinner." I shuddered, and Mrs. Pembroke asked if I was cold. She bought green peanuts for boiling, sweet potatoes and some turnips. She paid me and turned to walk away.

"Ma said tell you the fall collard greens will be in by next week if we get a little frost," I called. To Baldy, I said, "I hope you didn't hear what she said."

Mrs. Howard was my next customer and she bought the dozen brown shelled eggs Ma always saved for her. Then Mrs. Thompson came and bought all the pecans I had. I assured her there would be more next week.

On the way home, the money jingled in my pocket—two half dollars, four quarters and five dimes. Ma was pleased and said I'd make a good business woman when I grew up. When I told her Mrs. Pembroke tried to buy Old Baldy for her Christmas dinner, Ma looked thoughtful. I knew what a nuisance Ma thought Old Baldy was, and for a moment I was scared. Then she smiled and said we'd better go pick up pecans while the sun was still warm.

A row of pecan trees lined the property between our property and the Baxters next door. Some of the limbs hung over the fence, so the Baxters were entitled to the nuts that fell in their yard. When we got close to the first tree, Old Baldy gobbled loudly. He spied the Baxter boys and ran ahead of us, ready to fight them off if necessary. They scrambled over the fence so fast that they left the sack they'd been filling with our pecans. Ma estimated they'd saved us about 25 pounds worth of work.

A hobo appeared one day from the direction of the railroad tracks. When he opened our gate, Old Baldy was there in a flash. He quickly charged the hobo, screeching, flapping his wings and extending his feet to show off his dangerous spurs. Out the gate the hobo ran, mumbling to himself. Old Baldy returned to my side, looking proud of himself.

Pa finally made it home before Christmas. Ma told me to make sure the turkey remembered Pa before I let him loose in the yard. We didn't want Old Baldy to chase Pa off.

While I was washing the supper dishes that night, I heard Ma and Pa talking. She said, "Old Baldy is as good a watch dog as Tige ever was. Can you believe Mrs. Pembroke wanted to buy him for their Christmas dinner? As if we'd part with him for love or money!"

THE CHRISTMAS IT SNOWED
by Jenny Van Mill

[This story, published here for the first time, is about a rarity in Florida: snow on Christmas.]

The only snow we get in Florida is made of Styrofoam. It falls, predictably, shortly before Christmas on various Nutcrackers, Little Match Girls, and Christmas Carols. Well, it's not quite true that we never get the real stuff. About ten years ago—was it '89 or '90?—we did have snow, right here in Gainesville, Florida. It made the headlines. I still have that newspaper somewhere. We also saved a snowball—a dirty gray thing full of twigs that sat in the freezer for months because no one wanted to destroy evidence of the miracle. Snapper didn't think the snow was much of a miracle. Early that morning when Thomas and I took him out, he blinked snow out of his worried eyes and picked up his feet carefully, stopping every couple of minutes to shake snow off his coat. We took him into the woods across from the house where the snow was deeper and the fans of the palmettos were edged in white. Oblivious to the beauty, Snapper tucked his tail between his legs and refused to move. A strange and wonderful dog, Snapper. A bull terrier. A ferocious wimp.

I was not a wimp that day. Even though the radio announcer was telling us to stay off the roads, I was determined to get to church, not out of religious fervor but because I'm in the choir and we'd been practicing this anthem for weeks. My belief in God is nothing compared to my belief in singing. That's a terrible thing to say, but God doesn't seem to hold it against me. I believe singing releases just as many endorphins into the system as exercise, and it's a lot less painful. My voice is not spectacular—a music teacher once defined it as an "English soprano." Sometimes, nowadays, I threaten to quit the choir because sopranos are a dime a dozen, but after all these years it's hard to imagine Thursday nights without choir practice and Sunday mornings without the anthem, even though the choir is very lopsided at times—two dozen women jammed into the stalls on the pulpit side of the chancel opposite four men trying to fill up the pews in front of the organ. Why do women turn out in droves for such activities, while men must be courted and coddled? It was the same thing in ballet years ago. Men were exotics. Even those with little training or talent had to be cultivated with care.

It must have been a Sunday, then, the day the snow came. I know it was close to Christmas. The car door was frozen shut and I had to pour hot water on it to get it open. Thomas was watching from the front window, looking more like an anxious father than a son. I felt dizzy with the cold air and the whiteness. I drove to church at about 20 miles an hour and those of us out on the dangerous roads smiled at each other as though we were sharing a great adventure.

It's not that we don't get cold weather here in North Florida. We do, every year. The temperature dips into the twenties, the 'teens on rare occasions. But it always seems abnormal, an aberration, and the atmospheric conditions hardly ever conspire to produce snow. Whenever the temperature threatens to dip, the TV weatherman gives solemn instructions about protecting the "three Ps"—pets, plants, and pipes. Sometimes he adds a fourth P—people—and reminds us to wear hats and gloves if we go out, as though the Florida sun has addled our brains and we can't be trusted to know when our heads and hands are cold.

Of course, visiting snowbirds make fun of all this. They've left twelve feet of snow up north, impassable roads, and a power outage. Our short cold snaps are a joke. People from other countries—cold countries— laugh at us too. Well, I'm from another country myself—England—but I've lived in Florida since I was 17 and my blood's probably as thin as that of any native-born Floridian. Perhaps it was always thin. I don't think I ever got warm as a child, even in summer, which was sometimes practically non-existent. The English joke about their summers—"Wasn't summer on a Wednesday last year?" I can remember waking in the night freezing, clutching my no-longer-hot water bottle. I can remember the morning struggle, trying to get dressed under the bedclothes.

We didn't get much snow though, in that little coastal town. I don't know if we ever had a white Christmas. Surely I would remember something like that. What I do remember is my sister crying on Christmas morning. We always went to bed early on Christmas Eve. My mother gave each of us—Nora, John, and me—a clean white pillowcase to hang at the bottom of the bed, and some time in the night Father Christmas came and put a few toys in it, along with an apple, an orange and some nuts. On Christmas morning, my sister never found what she wanted in her pillowcase, and for the rest of Christmas Day she dragged it behind her, as miserable as old Marley with his chains. I wonder if that happened every year or just once. My sister would probably deny it ever happened at all. But I've often thought that what Nora was looking for on Christmas morning would never be found in a pillowcase. I think I know what she was looking for. It's the same thing I'm looking for myself.

At church that snowy day there was a sense of excitement. A lot of people had braved the elements to get there and they were noisy and happy, chatting in clusters, waving at each other. We crowded into the Parish Hall because the heating system in the church had shut down and those of us in the choir sat in front, just behind the makeshift altar. I think the sermon that Sunday cast some doubt on Mary's virginity but the congregation didn't seem to react—they were snow-shocked or reliving the brave moment that morning when they announced, "I don't care what the weatherman says—I am going to church." Or they may have tuned out when they saw the direction the sermon was taking. I often do that myself. These days I use the time to think about people who are dead—my mother and dad, my in-laws, Grandma, who came to live with us when I was two and stayed for ever, Snapper, who died three years ago, the two choir members who died last year. And of course my ballet teacher, Mrs. Pofahl, who said my arms were good—lovely *port de bras* was the way she put it—even though my turnout and extension left much to be desired. A friend wrote that as you get older, the time allotted in the service for remembering the dead isn't enough. That's true. I'm sixty-three and my list grows longer every year. I suppose I'll be on somebody else's list one day.

I was only in my early fifties the Sunday it snowed. I wish I'd known how young I was. Now I sound like my mother-in-law. *Dear, you just don't know how young you are.* She used to say that often, especially toward the end of her life when she seemed haunted by missed opportunities, unrealized dreams, and didn't want me to suffer the same regrets. She hadn't always worried about personal fulfillment, her own or mine. I know she considered it a waste of her son's hard-earned money (he did too) when I started taking ballet lessons at the age of 27. Didn't I have enough to do, with a house, a husband, and three children? And two years later, when Mrs. Pofahl allowed me into the ballet company, Mom just shook her head at such foolishness. But I think she was envious too.

Well, I thought everyone must be envious. There I was dancing on the stage of the University of Florida's Constans Theatre. I loved dancing in *The Nutcracker* best, especially the Saturday matinee, the children's show. I know there are people who find *The Nutcracker* boring, no matter how many new twists are added. I'm not too keen on watching it myself, particularly Act II, when Clara and the Nutcracker enter The Kingdom of the Sweets and along with the audience have to sit through an interminable series of character dances: "Marzipan Shepherdesses," "Chocolate," "Coffee," "Tea." *The Nutcracker* has always had its detractors. Years ago, in his *Complete Book of Ballets*, Cyril W. Beaumont wrote: "It passes the understanding . . . that 'Tea' should be suggested by a couple of ridiculous Chinese whose 'number' seems to have been borrowed from a pantomime version of Aladdin."

But *The Nutcracker* is a different thing altogether when you're dancing in it, when you're part of the magic. In Act I, I was Mother in a shimmering blue hoop-skirted dress I'd made myself. It was the only leading role I ever had, and I really got it by default: I was the only member of the company old enough to play a convincing Mother. *(I didn't know how young I was then, either, Mom.)* Outside it might be a muggy seventy-five degrees, but inside the theater it was cool, and I stood on the dark stage with Joe Tate, the electrician who'd been roped into playing Father by his daughter, who was our Clara. Mother and Father stood upstage in the dark in front of the huge Christmas tree that was made of green burlap and wood slats. We had to be careful not to trip over the thick part at the bottom, where the tree was folded upon itself accordion-style so that later, when ropes were pulled, it could magically grow. We hummed along with the overture, Joe and I, standing absolutely still as the stage lights began to come up and the curtain began to rise and we could hear the audience rustling and coughing, and children's voices. The bright lights brought us to life. We were Mother and Father preparing for the Christmas party, using large gestures to consult with each other on the placement of the final decorations on the tree.

When the tree was finished, Joe's daughter, Lynne, ran in to admire it. She was a perfect Clara, the child of every mother's dream, her red velvet dress guaranteeing that she would not get lost among the other children who were now beginning to enter stage right with their parents, all perfectly behaved, curtseying and bowing to Mother and Father, smilingly offering gifts to Clara and her brother Franz. Then Drosselmeyer arrived in a dramatic flourish of red-and-black cape and presented the nutcracker to Clara and planted a kiss on Mother's right hand.

My moment of glory came when the guests moved back and Mother and Father took center stage for their waltz, a dance that blessedly didn't require extension or turnout and allowed Mother to show off her lovely *port de bras.* It was all better than any real party I'd ever been to, far better than any I'd ever given. And the best thing was that after the party was over and the guests and their children had left the stage, the Christmas magic wasn't finished. It was just beginning.

I think that was why Nora cried when she stuck her head into the pillowcase—there was no Christmas magic in it, only presents. There was nothing to crown the weeks of anticipation when we had glued together miles of paper chains and cut "Happy Christmas" out of silver paper to stick on the mantelpiece mirror. And as soon as it got dark, we traipsed about the neighborhood, knocking on doors, singing carols for pennies with a candle in a jar, afterwards counting and recounting our money like gleeful Scrooges.

I loved being Mother, but I was always glad when Scene I came to an end, and I could rush to the dressing room to exchange the blue hoop skirt for a white tutu. Even Cyril W. Beaumont found something to admire in Scene II: "The scene of the snowflakes in which the fairies wave branched sticks tipped with fleecy balls of snow, and perform their evolutions amid falling snowflakes, is a charming spectacle." I've never liked the snowballs-on-sticks myself—they look too much like giant lollipops—and in our version we dispensed with them. With so many dancers on that small stage, I think Mrs. Pofahl was wise enough to realize that the addition of snow-sticks could have yielded disaster—or worse, farce. Of course I wasn't one of the main snowflakes, the ones who dazzled the audience with their *fouetté* turns and *grands jetés*. But even though my technique (or lack of it) placed me on the back row of the *corps de ballet,* my celebrated arms did earn me a coveted spot near the center. We held a pose while the Snow Queen did her solo, and I could look up at my right hand and see the imprint of Drosselmeyer's lipsticked kiss, which I never wiped away until the performance was over—it would have brought bad luck. At the end of the scene, we waved in unison on the swell of Tchaikovsky's music as Clara and her Nutcracker exited stage left, then lightly the snow began to fall and we rose to our toes and began turning and turning in the dim blue light, never stopping until the curtain was all the way down.

My sister never cried on Christmas Eve. The day before we had taken our Christmas caroling money and made our purchases. No more staring into shop windows for hours at fancy hankies and scarves and fur-lined gloves all surrounded by tinsel that just managed to hide the price tags. We had bravely opened the clanging shop door and summoned the shopkeeper from his tea. On Christmas Eve we wrapped the presents in tissue paper and hid them under the bed. Then we hung up our pillowcases and started waiting for Christmas, sitting next to the window even though we were freezing. You could feel that something wonderful was going to happen. The air felt full of secrets that were just about to be whispered into your ear.

From our window we couldn't see much of the sky, but Florence Birch's house across the street was almost as good. Their house was made of pebbledash—which meant that bits of colored glass were stuck in the walls. At night the glass sparkled like hundreds of tiny stars. When we were too cold to sit there any longer, we got into bed. Nora and John had told me long ago that there was no such thing as Father Christmas, that it was just something the grownups had made up, but on Christmas Eve I always thought they might be wrong. My ears were alert for the sound of sleigh bells, and every time I woke up in the night I went to the bottom of the bed to see if the pillowcase was lumpy yet.

But Christmas Eve is always full of promise. At the midnight service, when the air is heady with incense and the altar ablaze with poinsettias and candles, you sit in the choir stall and look out at the packed church and feel that anything is possible. The music is glorious, the choir has never sounded better, and the people passing on their way to take communion reach into the choir stalls to squeeze our hands. We're all part of a great brotherhood, we love each other, we love everyone, the world is going to be transformed. Jesus didn't die in vain!

The euphoria doesn't last of course. By the end of the service everyone's exhausted. In the choir room, we drink champagne and congratulate each other on another splendid Christmas service but the brotherhood can hardly wait to disband.

I think my sister discovered a terrible truth when she looked into her pillowcase: Christmas never comes. It's always coming but it never arrives. *Are you ready for Christmas?* turns into *Did you have a lovely Christmas?* and you daren't admit that nothing happened in the interim. You can come quite close to Christmas though, sometimes. I felt very close that Sunday ten years ago, when Thomas and I walked through the woods in the falling snow, laughing at poor Snapper as we coaxed him along. White dog against white snow—he looked like a cowardly miniature polar bear. The crisp cold air seemed alive with Christmas promise and I don't think it was just because of the snow. In church on Christmas Eve, you often feel the same way—right on the very brink of Christmas—surely it will come this year!—and it's only when you're in the choir room taking your first sip of champagne that you realize Christmas is over.

Maybe we're not ready for Christmas yet. For me, the closest I ever came was on the stage of the Constans Theatre, when I was a snowflake in a sparkly tiara and a classic white tutu, twirling and twirling in the blue light amidst the falling Styrofoam snow.

OCALA CHRISTMAS REMEMBERED
by Pauline Wood

[The following story, reprinted with permission from *Florida Living Magazine* (December 1985), depicts a simpler holiday celebration many years ago.]

My three brothers and I knew that we would not wake up on Christmas morning to find an abundance of various toys or expensive gifts but that did not put a damper on our feelings or love, much as the average child of that day and certainly as much as was good for us.

The anticipation, the simple gifts we received and the good food which Mama prepared was enough to make us happy. There were no electric trains, Barbie dolls, space ships, computers and other intricate toys that children receive in this modern age, nor did we have any use for little red sleds or ice skates. Our treasures brought by Santa were tops, marbles, horns, drums, iron trains, iron trucks, fire engines, books, roller skates and a Bisque doll or Rose O'Neill Kewpie doll for me, along with beautiful paper dolls.

We never bought a Christmas tree, but would cross Anthony Road and go into the woods which was just a short distance from our home at that time. But one Christmas Eve, Papa and I crossed Clerk Lane behind our home, walked down the Pear Lane, crossed North Sanchez Street, and went into the dense growth of brambles, bushes and trees in the swamp skirting Taylor's Pond, where the American Legion Home now stands, to find just the Christmas tree we wanted.

It was a beautiful large cedar. Papa cut it down and we dragged and lugged it home with much pulling, twisting, tugging and groaning on our part. Papa made a "stand" for it and placed it in the corner of the large dining room where we always stood our Christmas tree as the heater was in there and it was warm and cozy.

It reached the ceiling and we decorated it with garlands of red and green paper decorations twined around the tree. We didn't have any electric lights for the tree; in fact, I don't believe that they were being used by anyone at that time or that any even existed. Mama let us light candles on the tree on Christmas Eve for a short time while we were all in the room, but we had to be very careful and see that a candle did not turn over and catch the tree on fire.

Christmas Eve seemed to me when I was a child to be a time of awe, a time of mystery.

There was a quietness on the cold, starry twilight. There was an air of expectancy. At dusk we waited for the first lights to appear—far frosty stars covering the deepening sky. We would look into the cold, dark sky with twinkling stars and think of the Star that shone on that night so long ago, thinking of it as we had read about it and had sung the ever loved Christmas Carols proclaiming the Birth of Christ.

There was one memorable late Christmas Eve afternoon when my imagination ran riot.

Just at sundown I walked out of the kitchen where Mama was busy with pies, cakes and goodies, onto our back porch, which ran across the south side of the house. As I stepped out of the kitchen door, I looked to the west and the setting sun accentuated the different formations of the clouds. One large white cloud, outlined with the red of the setting sun, looked exactly like a large sleigh with a Santa sitting in it.

I stood transfixed and gazed at it for a long time until it dissolved and immediately as I looked over toward the street that ran behind our home, which was North Sanchez Street, again I saw something that looked like a large sleigh with a Santa and eight reindeer—Dasher, Dancer, Prancer, Vixen, Comet, Cupid, Donner and Blitzen—sailing along. It seemed as if Santa, his sleigh and eight helpers had descended from the sky and were scurrying down North Sanchez Street! How vivid and wonderful is the imagination of a child!

All through the years, as far back as I can remember, Christmas pageants were given on Christmas Eve in the old First Baptist Church on Magnolia Street in Ocala. The children and young people faithfully took part and memorized the parts assigned to them of Mary, Joseph, the Shepherds and the Wise Men.

How well do I remember one such unforgettable pageant on Christmas Eve. Mama and Papa took us to see and enjoy this little amateur performance to which we had all looked forward.

It was one of those cold, starlit nights, full of mystery and wonder, as only Christmas Eve can be to the very young. We found our seats and waited for the improvised curtain (a sheet) to be drawn back. Suddenly, there was the Bethlehem scene—the dark still night, the hillside, the Shepherds clutching their staffs, the papier-maché sheep, the gold foil star, the manger, Mary, Joseph, the Baby and the Wise Men bearing their gifts of Gold, Frankincense and Myrrh—all swathed in various coats, capes, scarfs, head pieces and mantles of many colors. It was all beautiful and exciting.

A little girl about my age, whose name was really "Fairy" and who lived in our block on Anthony Road, had a part in the Christmas pageant. On Christmas morning, the two of us were showing each other the gifts that Santa had brought us. When I saw that the doll truck which Santa had brought her was full of doll clothes and the doll truck which he brought me was empty I was heartbroken, even though it was a beautiful doll truck and I loved it—the luscious red plaid covering, the roomy interior and the pungent odor of the wood—I can still smell it, but I could not understand why Santa had slighted me and not brought me some doll clothes too.

My mother tried to console and explain to me that I already had a doll and doll clothes and that possibly Santa was just trying to be a little extra nice and give a little reward to the little girl because she had taken part in the Christmas pageant.

I suppose that every family observes Christmas rituals and ours was that on Christmas Eve Papa always hid the door key that locked the door between the living room and the dining room where the Christmas tree and gifts were.

When we got up on a cold, gray Christmas dawn, we had lots of fun searching frantically for that key and wondering what treasures lay under the Christmas tree behind the locked door. This was always an exciting time—the zest of anticipation, finding the key, bursting into the dining room and opening and exclaiming over the gifts—horns, tops, iron trains, trucks, fire engines, blocks, tinker toys, sparklers, pop corn, candy, oranges, apples and always a doll and a book for me.

Although I always loved and appreciated any gift that I received for Christmas, the one thing I treasured more than anything else was a book and that is what my Uncle Foy always gave me. I spent Christmas day enjoying everything else but always, in the back of my mind, was "the book" that I was saving for the last, when I could go off to my room by myself and positively "devour" it from cover to cover.

On Christmas morning, the first thing Papa said was "Christmas Gift!" as he first saw and greeted each member of the family as we walked into the room or to friends and neighbors who came by.

I never heard anyone else use this expression and never knew where it originated until years later in reading Civil War historical novels about the Old South.

I learned that this was the custom on Christmas morning. All of the slaves would leave their cabins and come up to Marse's Big House and they would all gather outside and call out "Christmas Gift!" Then the master and his wife and family would come out, wish all of the slaves a Merry Christmas and hand out gifts to them of clothing, extra food and toys for the children, most of them being handmade.

Gradually, the expression was handed down and other people took up the expression as a joke and tender of good will, as Papa did. After all, the Civil War had only been over about 50 years and many old Southern customs still prevailed. Anyhow, Papa enjoyed it and it was a part of his exuberant personality and we enjoyed his little joke too.

Some of my little girl friends invariably went to the picture show (as the Movie was called in those long ago days) on Christmas afternoon, but I don't believe that wild horses could have dragged me to a picture show—there was too much fun, frolic and excitement at home and I was afraid I would miss something, and besides I could go to a picture show any old time.

We thoroughly enjoyed every moment of Christmas Day—from the moment we hit the floor in the cold, dark morning, delved into our stockings hanging over the fireplace to find what goodies they held, to tearing around looking for the hidden key to all the treasures, looking at our gifts and exclaiming over them, then dashing out to compare everything we had gotten with the neighborhood kids. There has never been such a morning—noise, horns, drums, yells, screams, fire-crackers, sparklers, skates grinding up and down the street, and skinned knees from falling, laughter, squealing, balloons bursting, falling off of new bicycles, and collapsing in bed worn out but happy. Yes, every moment was sacred and to be stored in our minds as precious memories and cherished forever. No, I could not have gone to a picture show on Christmas Day.

I don't know how it is in other neighborhoods but in ours nowadays, Christmas morning is quiet as a death toll—not a sound anywhere, no happy children's voices, no noise of any kind. It is weird! Where has it gone? The noise, the fun, the laughter? What has happened? Where are the children? It's as quiet as if they had all followed the Pied Piper of Hamelin and his magic flute. Where is the magic and Christmas morning noise?

BIBLIOGRAPHY

Charles W. Arnade. *The Siege of St. Augustine in 1702.* Gainesville: University of Florida Press, 1959.

Randall Bedwell. *Christmas in the South: Yuletides Not Forgotten.* Nashville, TN: Spiridon Press, 1998.

Robert Chambers, editor. *The Book of Days.* London: W & P Chambers, 1878.

Christmas in Colonial and Early America. Chicago: World Book, Inc., 1996.

Jonathan Dickinson. *Jonathan Dickinson's Journal or God's Protecting Providence, Being the Narrative of a Journey from Port Royal in Jamaica to Philadelphia between August 23, 1696 and April 1, 1697.* Port Salerno, FL: Florida Classics Library, 1988.

J.W. Ewan, "The Seminole's Christmas," *Tequesta,* no. 40 (1980), pp. 39-42.

E.H. Gore. *From Florida Sand to "The City Beautiful."* Orlando: Orange Press, 1950.

Patricia C. Griffin. *Mullet on the Beach: The Minorcans of Florida, 1768-1788.* Jacksonville: University of North Florida Press, 1991.

Karl Grismer. *The Story of Fort Myers.* Fort Myers: Island Press, 1982.

W. Carew Hazlitt. *Faiths and Folklore.* New York: Charles Scribner's Sons, 1905.

Charles E. Kany. *Life and Manners in Madrid, 1750-1800.* Berkeley: University of California Press, 1932.

More Tales of Sebastian. Sebastian, FL: Sebastian River Area Historical Society, 1992.

Virginia Parks, editor. *Christmas in Old Pensacola.* Pensacola: Pensacola Historical Society, 1978.

Thelma Peters. *Lemon City: Pioneering on Biscayne Bay, 1850-1925.* Miami: Banyan, 1976.

Charles W. Pierce. *Pioneer Life in Southeast Florida.* Coral Gables: University of Miami Press, 1970.

Jane Quinn. *Minorcans in Florida: Their History and Heritage.* St. Augustine: Mission Press, 1975.

Marjorie Kinnan Rawlings. *Cross Creek.* New York: Scribner, 1942.

Eileen Ronan, "Christmas in Old St. Augustine," *North Florida Living,* December 1984, p. 35.

Julia Floyd Smith. *Slavery and Plantation Growth in Antebellum Florida, 1821-1860.* Gainesville: University of Florida Press, 1973.

Tywanna Whorley, "Harry Tyson Moore: A Soldier for Freedom," *Journal of Negro History,* vol. 79, no. 2 (1994), pp. 197-211.

Jerry Wilkinson, "Christmas in the Keys 1925," *Florida Keys Magazine,* December 1994, pp. 30-31.

INDEX

INDEX OF RECIPES

If you enjoyed reading this book, here are some other Pineapple Press titles you might enjoy as well. To request our complete catalog or to place an order, write to Pineapple Press, P.O. Box 3899, Sarasota, Florida 34230, or call 1-800-PINEAPL (746-3275). Or visit our website at www.pineapplepress.com.

Alligator Tales by Kevin M. McCarthy. True and tongue-in-cheek accounts of alligators and the people who have hunted them, been attacked by them, and tried to save them from extinction. Filled with amusing black-and-white photos and punctuated by a full-color section. ISBN 1-56164-158-8 (pb)

The Florida Chronicles by Stuart B. McIver. A series offering true-life sagas of the notable and notorious characters throughout history who have given Florida its distinctive flavor. **Vol. 1** *Dreamers, Schemers and Scalawags* ISBN 1-56164-155-3 (pb). **Vol. 2** *Murder in the Tropics* ISBN 1-56164-079-4 (hb)

Florida Fun Facts by Eliot Kleinberg. At last—a collection of every fact, large and small, that you need to know about Florida. Answers to questions like these: What's bigger, Lake Okeechobee or Rhode Island? What's wrong with Citrus County's name? And hundreds more! ISBN 1-56164-068-9 (pb)

Florida's Past, Volumes 1, 2, and *3* by Gene Burnett. Collected essays from Burnett's "Florida's Past" columns in *Florida Trend* magazine, plus some original writings not found elsewhere. Burnett's easygoing style and his sometimes surprising choice of topics make history good reading. ISBN **Vol. 1** 0-910923-27-2 (hb); 1-56164-115-4 (pb). **Vol. 2** 0-910923-59-0 (hb); 1-56164-139-1 (pb). **Vol. 3** 0-910923-84-1 (hb); 1-56164-117-0 (pb)

Florida Portrait: A Pictorial History of Florida by Jerrell Shofner. An in-depth reference—packed with hundreds of rare photographs—that chronicles Florida's history from the earliest Spanish explorers and Native American cultures to the space age and rampant population growth in the late twentieth century. ISBN 1-56164-121-9 (pb)

Guide to Florida Historical Walking Tours by Roberta Sandler.. Put on your walking shoes and experience the heart of Florida's people, history, and architecture as you take a healthful, entertaining stroll through 32 historic neighborhoods. ISBN 1-56164-105-7 (pb)

The Sunshine State Almanac and Book of Florida-Related Stuff by Phil Philcox and Beverly Boe. Chock-full of statistics, recipes, and photos, this handy reference is a veritable cornucopia of helpful and just plain fascinating stuff! Includes a long list of what's going on around Florida every month of the year. ISBN 1-56164-178-2 (pb)

You Got Me!—Florida by Rob Lloyd. Get an insider's grasp of the Sunshine State. Meticulously researched, this is a reference that will tickle your funny bone and tease your brain at the same time. ISBN 1-56164-178-2 (pb)